iCanPlayMusic

Complete Guitar Course

The definitive full-color picture guide to playing guitar

AMSCO PUBLICATIONS
part of the MUSIC SALES GROUP
New York/London/Paris/Sydney/Copenhagen/Berlin/Tokyo/Madrid

M000107760

Exclusive Distributors:
Music Sales Corporation
257 Park Avenue South
New York, NY 10010 USA

Music Sales Limited
14–15 Berners Street
London W1T 3LJ England

Music Sales Pty Limited
20 Resolution Drive,
Caringbah, NSW 2229, Australia.

Order No. AM 992200
International Standard Book Number: 978-0-8256-3591-5

This book © Copyright 2008 by Amsco Publications,
A Division of Music Sales Corporation, New York
www.musicsales.com

Cover design by Fresh Lemon
Edited by Sorcha Armstrong
Book design by Chloë Alexander
Music processed by Paul Ewers
Text photographs by George Taylor and Geoff Green
Models: Jim Benham, Arthur Dick, Andrew King, Ross Greening,
and David Bradley

Part One
Written and arranged by Arthur Dick
CD mastered by Jonas Persson
Guitars by Arthur Dick
Bass by Paul Townsend
Drums by Ian Thomas
Additional programming by John Moores

Part Two
Written and arranged by Joe Bennett
CD produced by Paul Morris
Guitars and bass by Joe Bennett
Drums by Mark Anderson

Printed in China

Contents

CD contents

iCanPlayMusic

Complete Guitar Course

PART ONE

Introduction

Welcome to *iCanPlayMusic: Guitar*.
The guitar remains one of the world's most popular instruments—this book will guide you from the very first time you take your guitar out of its case, to playing your first song.

Easy-to-follow instructions
will guide you through:

• how to look after your guitar
• how to tune it
• learning your first chords
• playing your first song

Play along with the backing track as you learn—the specially recorded audio will let you hear how the music should sound—then try playing the part yourself.

Practice regularly and often. Twenty minutes every day is far better than two hours on the weekend with nothing in between. Not only are you training your brain to understand how to play the guitar, you are also teaching your muscles to memorize certain repeated actions.

There are two main types of guitar.

The acoustic guitar has a hollow body that allows the sound of the vibrating string to be transmitted through the round soundhole.

Most electric guitars have solid bodies, so the string vibration is not particularly audible—that's why they have to be plugged into an amplifier.

Although the sound and character of acoustic and electric guitars are quite different, the principle workings are the same.

Electric

Acoustic

headstock

tuning pegs

nut

frets

fingerboard

strap attachment

strings

body

pick-ups

pick-up selector

bridge

volume/tone controls

headstock

tuning pegs

nut

frets

fingerboard

strings

soundhole

body

bridge

Know your guitar

The headstock (at the end of the fretboard) has six tuning pegs, either three each side or all six in a row.

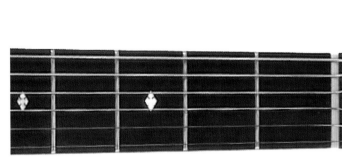

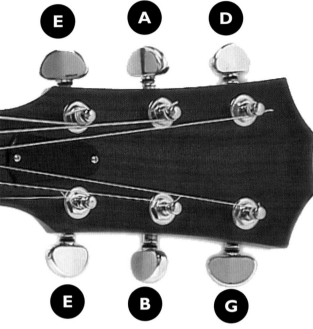

The tuning pegs, or machine heads, consist of a metal capstan and a cog to tension the string.

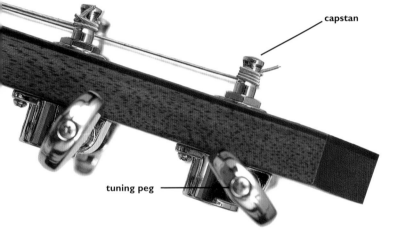

capstan

tuning peg

The strings are kept in place by the nut as they leave the headstock.

The strings traverse the fretboard (usually rosewood or maple) which may have plastic or tortoiseshell inlays to help you see where you are on the neck.

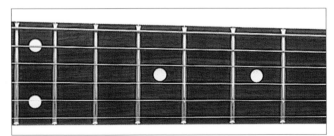

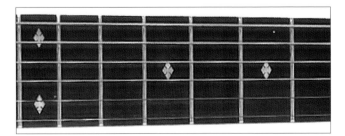

There are dots on the side of the neck at given fret positions as well.

The strings are attached to the body at the bridge, which comes in all shapes and sizes depending on the guitar, but in all cases acts to alter the harmonics and string height.

The bridge on an acoustic guitar is normally fixed and is therefore not adjustable, but on electrics a wide range of string adjustments can usually be made.

▲ Bridge — electric guitar

▲ Bridge — acoustic guitar

Below the strings and bridge, most electric guitars have controls for volume and tone.

The pick-up selector on the Les Paul type guitar is positioned above the strings; on the Fender Stratocaster type it can be found below.

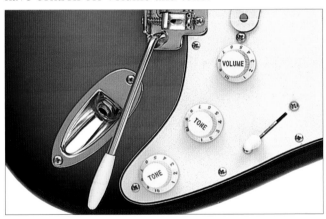

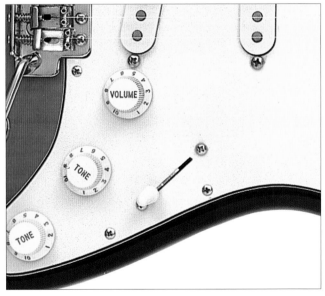

Most electric guitars come with a strap attachment.

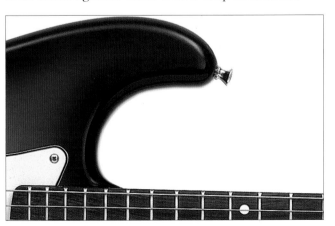

Strings and things

There is nothing quite like the tone of new strings on your guitar, but that sound will soon fade. Strings are made from alloy and tarnish easily, thus losing tone. To extend their life always wipe down the instrument at the end of each playing session, taking special care with the strings. A clean dry linen or silk cloth wiped over the strings will remove dirt and moisture.

Professional guitarists have a "guitar tech" or "roadie" to change strings for them—they're on hand throughout a gig in case a string breaks during the performance. It's their job to make sure all the guitars are in tune and set up in exactly the right way for that guitarist.

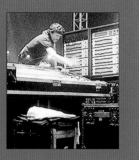

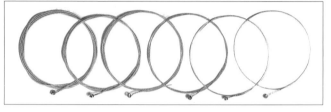

Strings vary in thickness from the bottom (thickest) to the top (thinnest). The bottom three are wound to give the sound more depth; the top three are just unwound alloy wire. When it's time to change your strings always check you have the right gauges.

The diameter of a string—its gauge—is measured in inches or centimeters: the lower the number, the thinner the string. A set of light gauge strings (0.09 - 0.42) may be preferable for electric guitar because it makes string-bending easier. A classical or Spanish guitar is intended to have nylon strings, in contrast to its steel-string relative, the folk acoustic guitar. If in doubt, consult your local music shop.

Following some simple guidelines will ensure that you always feel comfortable when playing.

1 Your arms should never take the weight of the guitar; they should be free just to play it.

2 Always keep the neck pointing slightly above the horizontal. Never let it point down toward the ground.

3 When practicing, it's more comfortable to sit down. Some players cross their legs right over left and rest the guitar on the right thigh, which elevates the instrument slightly.

Tip

Classical players have a seating posture of their own, using a footstool to raise the left foot, with the guitar tucked between the legs.

4 If you stand, you should not be supporting the guitar. Adjust the strap so the guitar is at a sensible height and position it so there is an equal balance of weight. When you take your hands away it should sit comfortably.

13

The electric guitarist

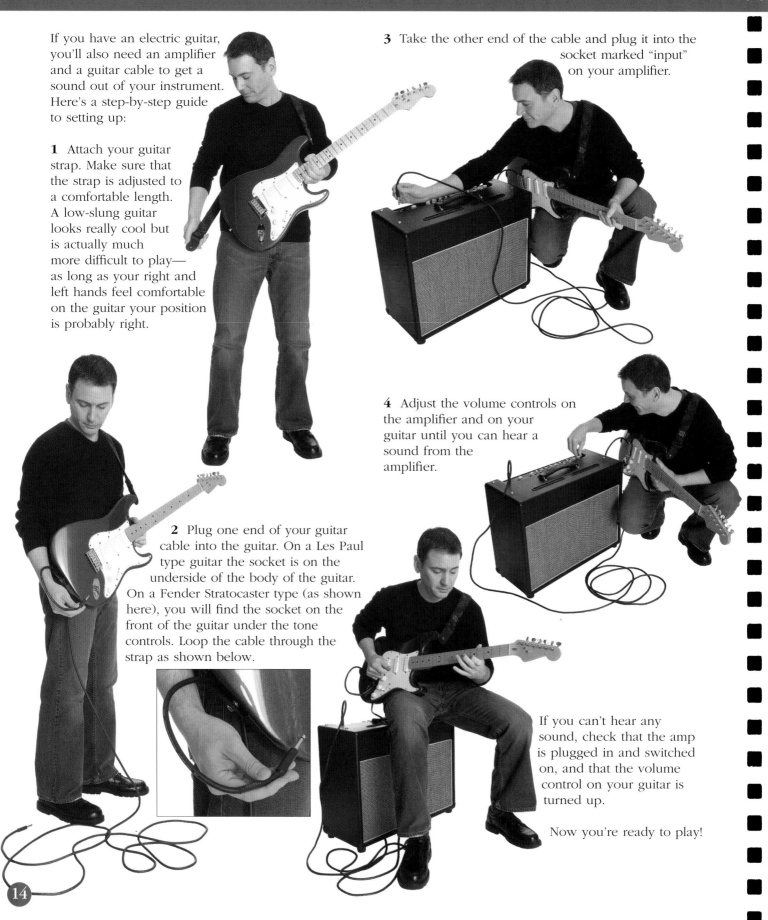

If you have an electric guitar, you'll also need an amplifier and a guitar cable to get a sound out of your instrument. Here's a step-by-step guide to setting up:

1 Attach your guitar strap. Make sure that the strap is adjusted to a comfortable length. A low-slung guitar looks really cool but is actually much more difficult to play—as long as your right and left hands feel comfortable on the guitar your position is probably right.

2 Plug one end of your guitar cable into the guitar. On a Les Paul type guitar the socket is on the underside of the body of the guitar. On a Fender Stratocaster type (as shown here), you will find the socket on the front of the guitar under the tone controls. Loop the cable through the strap as shown below.

3 Take the other end of the cable and plug it into the socket marked "input" on your amplifier.

4 Adjust the volume controls on the amplifier and on your guitar until you can hear a sound from the amplifier.

If you can't hear any sound, check that the amp is plugged in and switched on, and that the volume control on your guitar is turned up.

Now you're ready to play!

If you're lucky enough to have an effects unit such as a distortion or wah-wah pedal, you can have even more fun!

Effects pedals take the sound from your guitar and change it before it gets passed on to the amplifier. They can be powered by batteries or by a separate AC adaptor.

A wah-wah pedal produces a classic effect that you'll recognize instantly. You plug it in the same way as other effects pedals, and then vary the tone of your guitar sound by rocking back and forth on the pedal.

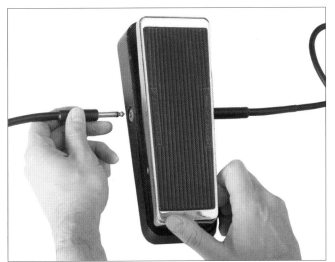

Take the other end of the cable that is plugged into your guitar and insert it into the input socket on the pedal (sometimes marked "instrument").

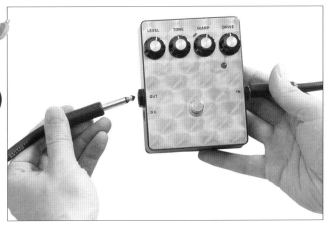

Then take another cable; insert one end of it into the pedal socket marked "output" (or "amplifier") and the other end into the input socket on your amplifier.

The pedal is activated by simply stomping on the foot-operated switch. When the pedal is not switched on you should still be able hear the sound of your guitar as before—when you step on the switch the sound should change as the effect kicks in.

Once you're happy with your guitar set-up, turn up the volume and make some noise!

Right-hand position

Your right hand can strum chords or pick single notes or you could use a pick. The best way to start is to strum the strings. Either use a soft (bendy) pick or hold your thumb and first finger together as though you had an imaginary pick. Rest your forearm on the guitar so it can swing freely. Get used to the feel of your strumming hand against the strings.

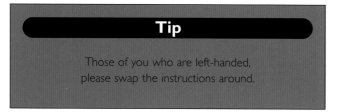

Tip

Those of you who are left-handed, please swap the instructions around.

As an exercise, just strum the strings downwards from the 6th (lowest in pitch) to the 1st.

Then strum down again but go from the 4th to the 1st, skipping over the 5th and 6th.

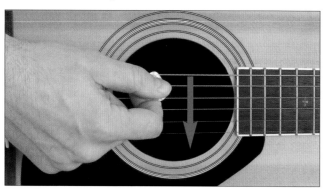

Once you're happy with the strumming motion, you can try finger-picking individual strings. The right hand adopts the following position:

1 Rest your forearm lightly on the guitar.

2 Arch your wrist so your fingers are approximately at 60 degrees to the back of your hand, then relax them so they become slightly curved.

Your right-hand technique might depend on the sort of music you want to play. Folk and country players tend to strum (without a pick) or finger-pick, whereas rock guitarists use a pick for maximum volume! However, some rock guitarists, like Mark Knopfler, prefer to use their fingers to create a distinctive sound.

3 Place your thumb (p) on the 6th string, your index finger (i) on the 3rd string, your middle finger (m) on the 2nd string and your ring finger (a) on the 1st string. Try to make sure that your thumb comes in contact with the strings about an inch or so in front of your index finger.

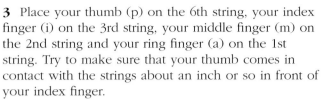

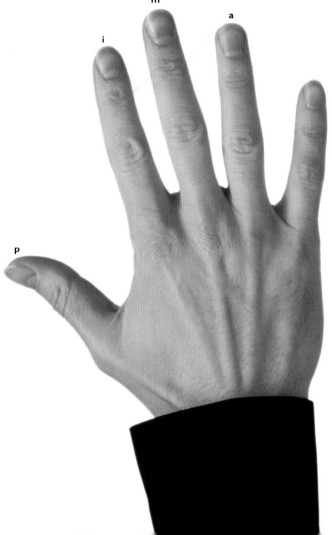

Holding the pick

The pick is held between the thumb and index finger of your strumming hand, which should be (roughly) at right angles to each other. Try out a few sizes and thicknesses of pick to find one you're comfortable with. Hold the pick securely and don't have too much of it protruding from your fingers toward the strings.

At first the pick may seem awkward, but this feeling will fade, and it will become an extension of your hand.

Play the open strings one at a time from the 6th to the 1st, then from the 5th to the 1st, 4th to the 1st and so on. Your pick should be hitting the upper side of each string and traveling toward the floor. This is known as a *downstroke*.

Now try strumming across the open strings with the pick—don't worry about your left hand at this stage, just get used to the sensation of the pick traveling across the strings.

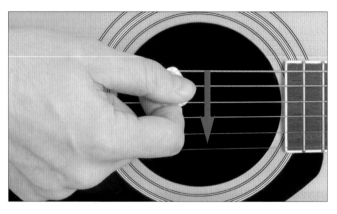

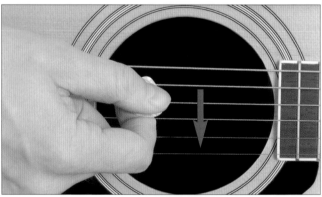

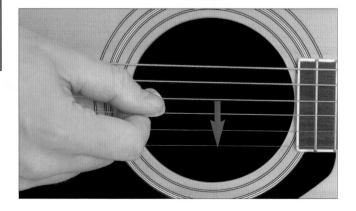

Tip

Playing live can be a nerve-wracking experience— it's very easy to drop your pick in the heat and sweat of a rock gig. Pro players stick spare picks to the back of their guitar, or wedge them under the pick-guard in case of emergencies!

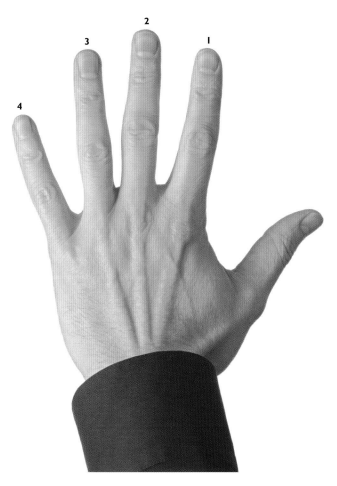

The first time you try a new chord you may find it hard to get the positioning of your fingers right, let alone press them down. If necessary, use your other hand to physically put each fretting finger in position.

The fretting fingers are numbered 1, 2, 3 and 4.

Try to keep the left hand relaxed. The left-hand thumb should be roughly vertical behind the neck and roughly behind the 1st and 2nd fingers.

Once you feel confident holding your guitar, experiment with different playing positions to see what feels the most comfortable. Almost every conceivable playing position has been used at some point—although some are more difficult than others!

Tip

The first few weeks will be tough on your fingers. But don't worry! Gradually you'll develop pads of harder skin on the ends of each finger. You'll need to keep practicing to make sure they don't disappear!

CHECKPOINT

WHAT YOU'VE ACHIEVED SO FAR...

You can now:
- Hold your guitar comfortably
- Name each part of the guitar
- Strum with fingers or with a pick
- Choose appropriate strings for your guitar

Tuning your guitar

There are various ways of tuning the guitar—use the one that suits you best.

Tuning to another instrument
The simplest way to make sure that your guitar is in tune is to find someone else with a tuned guitar and match each string on your guitar with the relevant string on the tuned guitar.

Tip

If you're playing with other people it's vital that you all tune to the same note. If one of the instruments can't be easily tuned (like a piano for example), make sure that you tune to that.

Alternatively, you could tune to a piano or electronic keyboard.

Refer to the diagram below to tune each string.

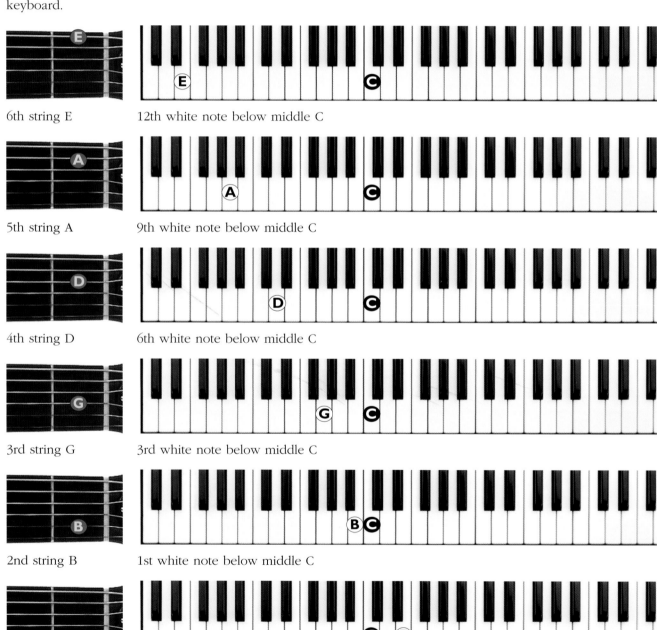

6th string E   12th white note below middle C

5th string A   9th white note below middle C

4th string D   6th white note below middle C

3rd string G   3rd white note below middle C

2nd string B   1st white note below middle C

1st string E   2nd white note above middle C

Tip

If you're not sure whether a note is sharp or flat (i.e. too high or too low), loosen the string being tuned a little and slowly bring it up to the required pitch.

This is perhaps the commonest method and one that works if you are pretty confident that at least one of the strings is in tune. Let's assume the bottom string (6th) is in tune. Being the thickest, you'll find that the 6th string probably won't drift out of tune as much as some of the others.

Follow the tuning diagram and tune from the bottom string upwards.

To tune:

| 6th to 5th string | 5th to 4th string | 4th to 3rd string | 3rd to 2nd string | 2nd to 1st string |

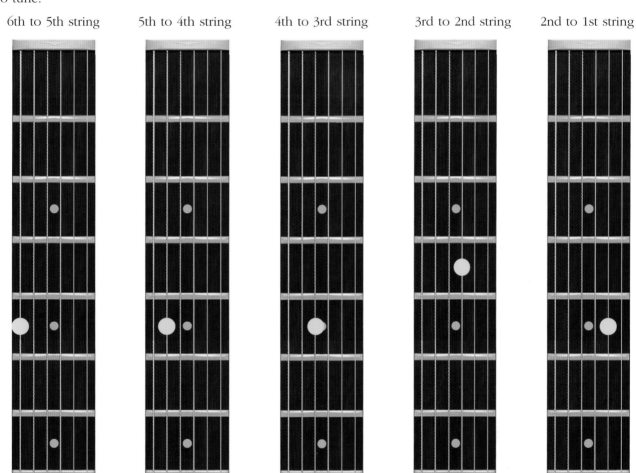

Track 1 of the CD gives tuning notes for each string, beginning with the 6th (lowest).

CHECKPOINT

WHAT YOU'VE ACHIEVED SO FAR...

You can now:
• Tune your guitar to a keyboard
• Use relative tuning
• Ensure that you are in tune with other musicians

Now that you've tuned up, let's play some chords. Besides learning the chord fingering, we're going to look at some simple strumming and work all the ideas into a song for you to play along with.

Compare how A looks in the photo to the chord box:

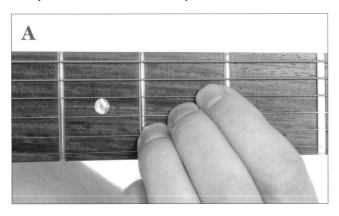

Chords for the guitar are pictured in the form of a "chord box," where the six strings are viewed as though you're looking at the guitar neck face on, with the strings going down the page. The numbers in circles tell you which fingers to use.

X = don't play this string
O = open string

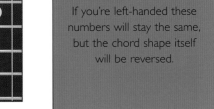

Tip

If you're left-handed these numbers will stay the same, but the chord shape itself will be reversed.

1 The fingers are placed just behind the 2nd fret. You never press down a string with a finger actually on the metal fret.

2 The fingers are angled to fit comfortably alongside each other and to fit in the narrow space.

3 The 6th string is not played; the 5th and 1st strings are "open" (i.e. not fretted and shown as 0 in the chord box).

4 Keep the little finger out of the way so it doesn't catch the 1st string.

Now strum the whole chord—just downward strums at first.

Track 2 demonstrates how the A chord should sound.

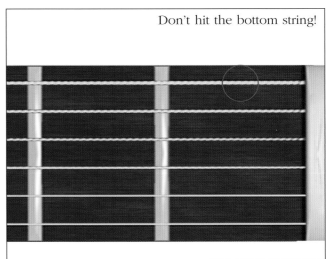

Don't hit the bottom string!

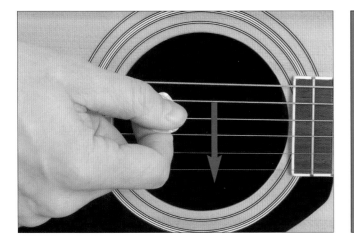

A major facts:

1 The A chord's full name is A major—later on you'll come across other types of A chords such as minor and seventh.

2 The A chord is named after its lowest note—the open A string (the 5th string).

3 Like all major chords, A major is characterized by a bright, happy sound.

The number in the circle tells you which left-hand finger to use.

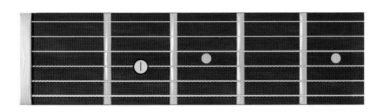

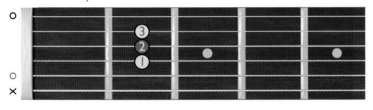

Final chord shape

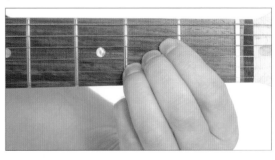

X = don't play this string   **O** = open string

Tip

Make sure you can hear all the notes clearly.
First play each string separately. If there is a buzz then something is wrong with the way you're holding down the note, or one of your other fingers is touching the adjacent string and preventing it from ringing as it should. You may have to press harder to get rid of the buzz, or, if you can, move your finger slightly closer to the fret. Experiment until you can hear all the strings in the chord sounding.

The chord of D

Let's try the D chord next. It only has four notes, so don't play the E and A (6th and 5th) strings.

1 The 3rd finger must avoid touching the E string (1st string) for all the strings to sound clearly.

2 Keep your little finger out of the way as it can clutter the hand position.

3 Play the strings separately from bottom to top (4th to 1st) and make sure they are all sounding clearly.

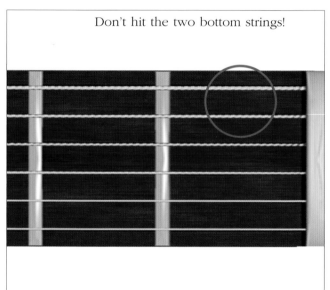

Don't hit the two bottom strings!

You have now learned two of the most common chords in pop—A and D. These two chords sound great when played one after the other—you'll find this chord change in hundreds of classic songs.

4 Now strum the whole chord.

Listen to **Track 3** to hear how the chord should sound.

D major facts:

1 The D chord is named after its lowest note—the open D string (the 4th string).

2 D is a favorite with folk guitarists—try adding your fourth finger at the third fret on the top string to form a chord of Dsus4, for a classic folky sound.

3 D and A sound great when played after each other.

The number in the circle tells you which left-hand finger to use.

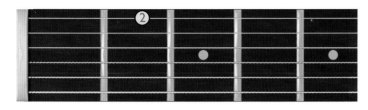

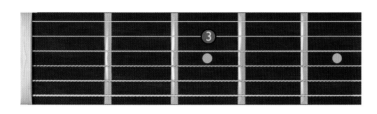

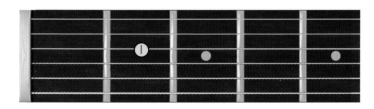

Final chord shape

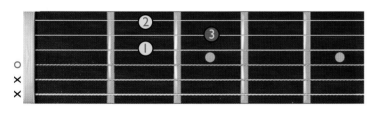

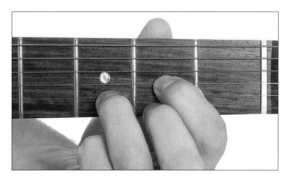

X = don't play this string   **O** = open string

Don't press down too hard with the fingers of your left hand—you'll be surprised how little pressure it actually takes to fret a chord successfully. Positioning your thumb comfortably behind the neck can be helpful.

The chord of E

This chord has inspired many classic riffs and songs, and sounds great because you can play all six strings. There are just three strings to fret (5th, 4th, and 3rd):

E is a powerful sounding chord because all six strings are played—including the open E strings which ring out.

Listen to **Track 4** to hear how it should sound.

1 Although the E chord is a relatively simple shape, be careful not to catch your 3rd finger on the 3rd string—this will stop the note ringing. Your end finger joints should adopt more of a vertical position above the string to avoid this.

2 Relax the thumb and arch the wrist for the best position.

E major facts:

1 The E chord is the fullest sounding of all the chords you've learned so far—because, unlike A or D, it uses all six strings.

2 E is possibly the most popular key for guitar music, because it allows you to use the open E strings (top and bottom strings).

3 Once you've perfected the E shape, try adding your little finger at the 2nd fret, 3rd string, to form the chord of Esus4.

▼ **The Jimi Hendrix classic "Hey Joe" relies heavily on the chord of E**

The number in the circle tells you which left hand finger to use.

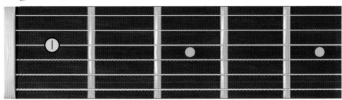

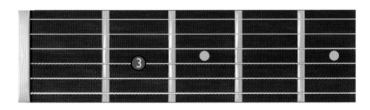

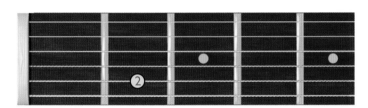

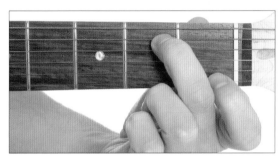

Final chord shape

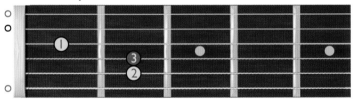

X = don't play this string   **O** = open string

A, D & E—the three-chord trick

The chords of A, D & E can be played in almost any sequence and they will still sound good.

In fact, lots of classic rock songs can be played using only these three chords—check out "Wild Thing," "Peggy Sue," or just about any blues tune to hear the three-chord trick in action.

CHECKPOINT

WHAT YOU'VE ACHIEVED SO FAR...

You can now:
• Play the chords of A, D and E major
• Strum 4, 5 or 6 string chords

Let's play!

Now that you're familiar with the chord shapes of A, D and E, let's do some playing!

In rhythm with A
Let's return to the chord of A. It doesn't matter whether you use a pick or not—but can you strum downward from the 5th string to the 1st without any buzzes?

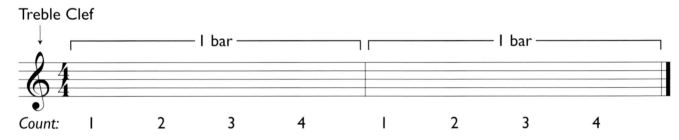

Treble Clef

I bar — I bar

Count: 1 2 3 4 1 2 3 4

There are two tracks on the CD for each example given here. The first is a full version with guitar; the second has the same backing but without the guitar part, so that you can play along. You'll soon get used to strumming in time with the music and eventually you'll be able to perform a smooth chord change with no problems.

Don't worry about the musical notation at this stage—later we'll use a very simple system to indicate rhythm but for now all you need to concentrate on is counting four beats per bar, as indicated below the staff.

The next example (see page 29) will get you started, with the chord of A!

Tip

The ⌐ means that you should strum each chord with a "downstroke," moving from the strings nearest the top of the guitar downwards toward the ground.

28

Track 5 starts with four clicks to give you the tempo. The track is just one bar repeated over and over, with the first beat accented, or played louder, so you can spot the start of each bar. Strum the A chord on the first beat of the bar.

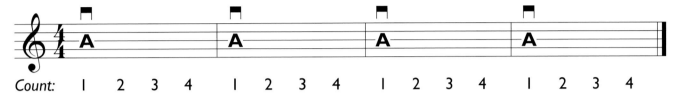

Count: 1   2   3   4   1   2   3   4   1   2   3   4   1   2   3   4

⊓ = downstroke

Sometimes it helps to count aloud while playing—alternatively you can tap your foot on the beat.

Track 6 gives you a chance to play along with the band.

Now let's play the same A chord twice per bar instead of once. Count four beats in a bar, and then strum the A chord as you count "one" and "three."

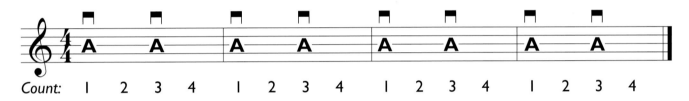

Count: 1   2   3   4   1   2   3   4   1   2   3   4   1   2   3   4

Track 7 demonstrates how this should sound.

Track 8 is your chance to go solo!

And now let's strum the A chord on each beat—use a downstroke as you count the four beats in each bar.

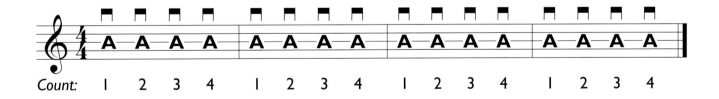

Count: 1   2   3   4   1   2   3   4   1   2   3   4   1   2   3   4

Track 9 demonstrates strumming on each beat.

Track 10 gives you the track minus the recorded guitar part, this time with no accents. Accent the first beat of each bar as you strum.

Upstroke/downstroke

The final strumming pattern requires you to strum up as well as down. Practice strumming as before with downstrokes, and then gradually try to catch the strings as you raise your hand back up again to strum downwards.

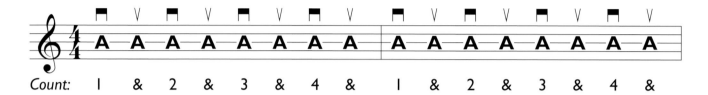

Count: 1 & 2 & 3 & 4 &   1 & 2 & 3 & 4 &

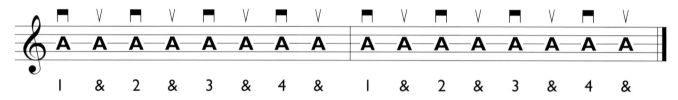

1 & 2 & 3 & 4 &   1 & 2 & 3 & 4 &

⊓ = downstroke
V = upstroke

These "upstrokes" occur between the beats: count **1** & **2** & **3** & **4** & throughout the bar—downstrokes should fall on the numbers, and upstrokes should fall on the "&"s.

When you hear **Track 11**, it will be obvious what's happening. However, continue to count the main beats as you strum and accent the first beat of each bar.

Track 12 is the backing track with only the first beat accented. Listen to the hi-hat in the drum part—that's the rhythm that you need to follow—and then try playing along.

1 Try to find time to practice every day—even if it's only for 10 minutes. It's much better to practice every day for 10 minutes than it is to practice once a week for two hours!

2 Identify chord shapes and techniques that you find difficult and practice them slowly and deliberately.

3 Pick each string of the chord and make sure that it is ringing out clearly before you start strumming.

In rhythm with D

Now that you are familiar with the A chord, let's also practice strumming the D and E chords you have learned.

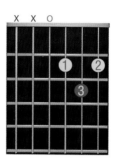

Listen to **Track 13** (with four clicks intro) and then strum once per bar on beat 1 along with **Track 14**.

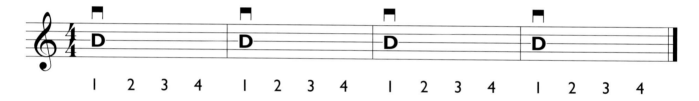

Track 15 demonstrates two strums of D on beats 1 and 3.

Play along with **Track 16**.

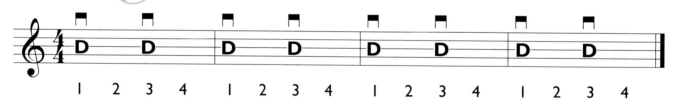

Now play four D chords in each bar, using a downstroke on each beat.

Listen to **Track 17** to hear how it should sound, and then try over the backing in **Track 18**.

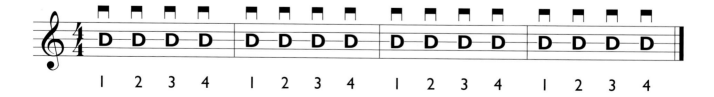

Track 19 uses downstrokes and upstrokes in continuous rhythm.

Track 20 is the backing track with the first beat of each bar accented.

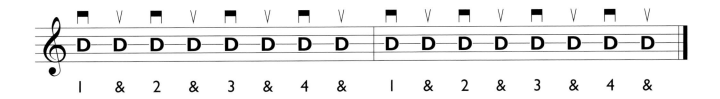

Remember you only need to strum the top four strings to make the chord of D—the bottom two strings should be avoided.

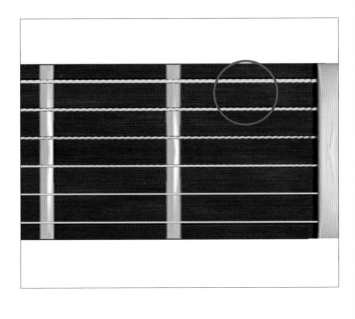

In rhythm with E

Here are the same exercises on the E chord.

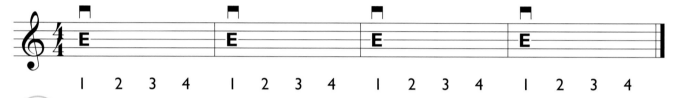

Track 21 demonstrates one strum of E per bar (remember the four clicks of the intro).

Track 22 is the backing track with an accent on beat 1.

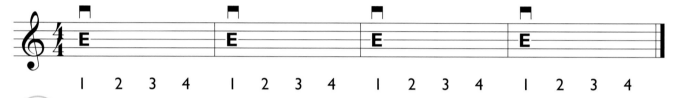

Track 23 has two strums per bar on beats 1 and 3.

Track 24 is the backing track with accents on beats 1 and 3.

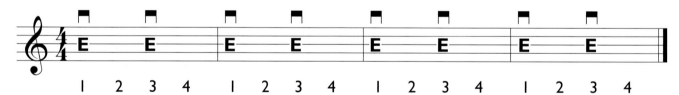

Track 25 requires four strums of E, one per beat of the bar, all downstrokes.

Track 26 is the backing track with accents on beat 1.

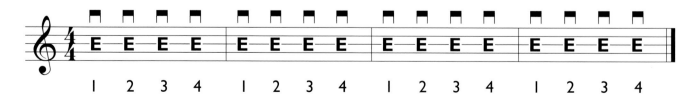

Track 27 uses downstrokes and upstrokes in continuous rhythm.

Track 28 is the backing track with the first beat of each bar accented.

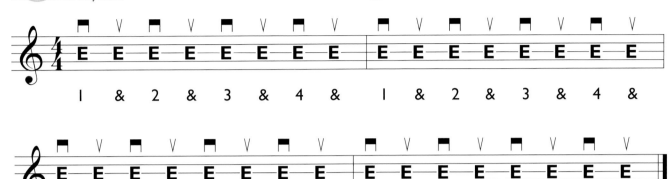

1 & 2 & 3 & 4 & 1 & 2 & 3 & 4 &

1 & 2 & 3 & 4 & 1 & 2 & 3 & 4 &

A

D

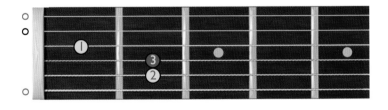

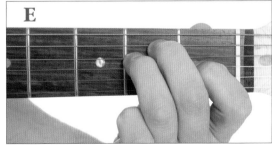

E

CHECKPOINT

WHAT YOU'VE ACHIEVED SO FAR...

You can now:
- Strum three major chords in time with backing tracks using upstrokes and downstrokes
- Follow a basic musical score

Moving around!

Now it's time to try changing chords from bar to bar.

For **Track 29** let's use only downstrokes and play one chord per bar.

A

D

E

A

Repeat Sign:
Repeat all 4 bars

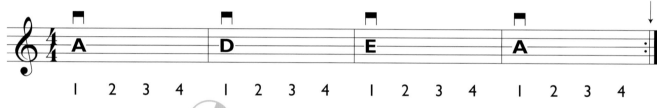

Now try playing with backing **Track 30**. Think ahead and prepare the next chord shape as soon as you've played the previous one.

Now try two strums per chord—i.e. on beats 1 and 2 of each bar. This leaves you the duration of beats 3 and 4 to change to the next shape. Can you feel when to change chord?

Once you've perfected two strums per bar, try moving up to three chords per bar (on beats 1, 2 and 3). This only gives you one beat to change between chord shapes!

Listen to **Track 31** to hear how this should sound, and then try yourself over the backing **Track 32**.

repeat

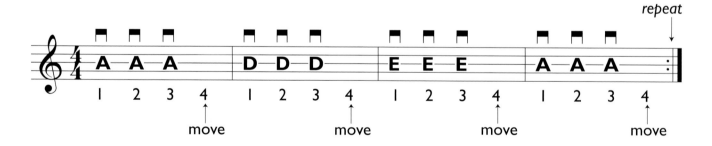

Tip

If you can't change chords fast enough initially, just ignore the strumming and simply move from one chord to the next in your own time until it feels comfortable.

The next step is to play the upstrokes as well.

First, strum beats 1 and 2 with down- and upstrokes and change chord shapes during beats 3 and 4.

Then, with **Track 32**, strum beats 1, 2 and 3 and change during beat 4.

Finally, try strumming up and down on beats 1, 2, 3 and 4, changing chord shape quickly before the start of the next bar.

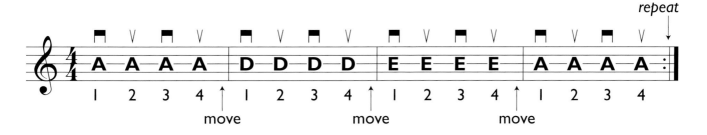

The objective is to make the chord changes as quick and smooth as possible. Try to strum for longer and longer, leaving less and less time for your left hand to change shape.

Eventually, you will be strumming 8 times a bar (4 up and 4 down) and you'll have to change shape in between the last upstroke of one bar and the first downstroke of the next one.

Listen to **Track 33** to hear how this should sound.

Track 34 is the backing track. A crash cymbal indicates the beginning of the four bar pattern.

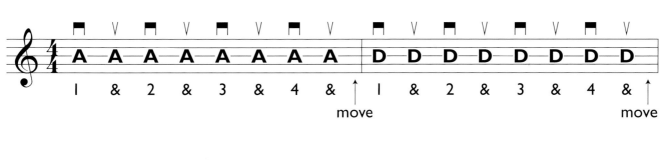

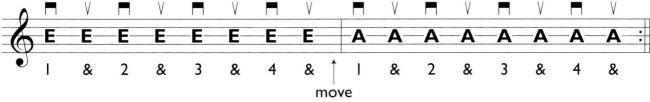

The chord of G

To play the song that follows you need two extra chords, G and C.

Notice how the 1st and 2nd fingers arch over to come down on the strings so as to avoid catching the open strings.

To hear how it should sound, check out **Track 35**.

To practice G, try these exercises. First, strum the G chord on the first beat of the bar only.

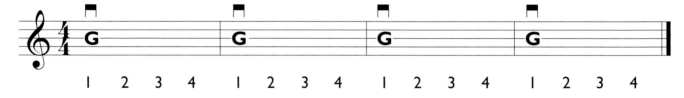

Listen to **Track 36** to hear how this sounds.

Track 37 is the backing track with only the first beat of each accented.

The next pattern uses up and down strumming—count steadily and try to keep your strumming arm relaxed as you play.

Tip

Use the same strum patterns as you have been practicing to get used to strumming the new chord of G.

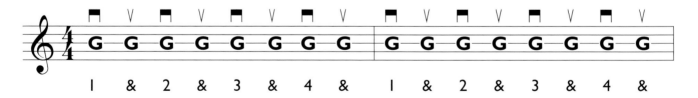

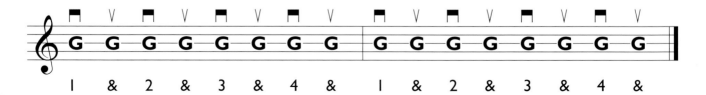

38

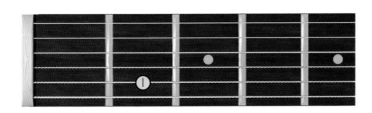

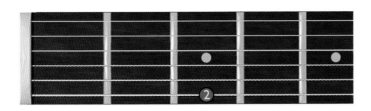

Final chord shape

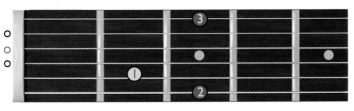

O = open string

Once again, care must be taken not to muffle the open fourth and second strings with the fretting fingers.

The chord of C

This chord is slightly more difficult than the four you have already learned, because an open string is hidden in the middle of the chord shape.

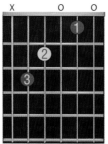

The first finger has to be almost vertical to clear the 1st string, so make sure your nails are short enough to press down onto the 2nd string in this way. Watch out that you don't catch your 2nd finger against the open 3rd string (G).

Track 38 demonstrates how it sounds—make sure you don't strike the bottom string!

Now strum the chord against the rhythm track, one strum per bar.

Do not play the 6th string!

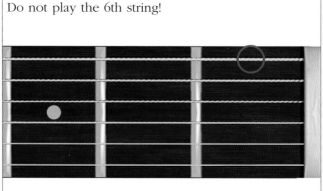

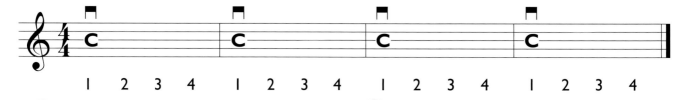

Track 39 demonstrates how this example should sound.

Track 40 is your chance to practice your strumming technique.

Now try strumming up- and downstrokes, accenting the first beat each time.

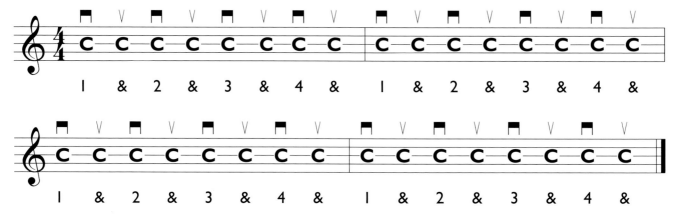

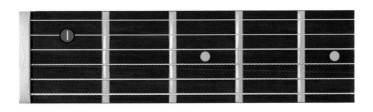

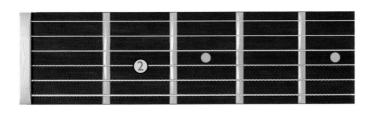

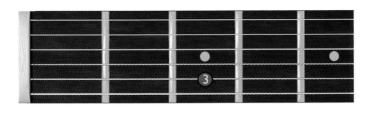

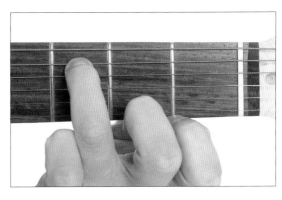

Final chord shape

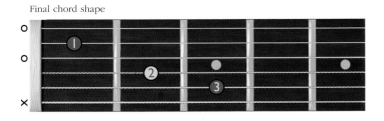

X = don't play this string   O = open string

Be careful not to catch the open third string with your second finger, and similarly, don't muffle the open top string with your first finger.

Once again, if you attempt to make your fingers meet the fingerboard at right angles you shouldn't have any problems.

Your first song

Now let's take all five chords and play a complete song!

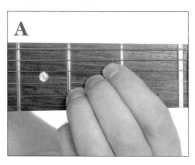

A

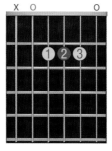

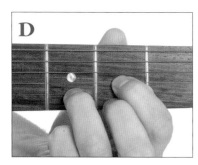

D

E

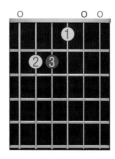

G

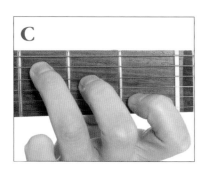

C

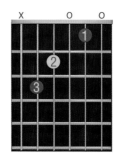

Listen to **Track 41** and follow the musical example opposite until you are familiar with all the chord sequences in the song.

Understanding musical notation
Don't be put off by the musical signs we've used here—this is how it works:

1 Play through the **Intro** in exactly the same way as you have played all the other examples in this book—count steadily and play the chords as indicated.

2 Play through the **Solo/melody** until you come to the :‖ sign—that's a repeat sign, and it means you have to go back to A and play that section again.

3 The second time through don't play the bars under the number 1 but go straight to the bars under the number 2.

4 Ignore the **To Coda ⊕** sign for the time being and play right on into the next section—there's another repeat here.

5 Once you've repeated that sequence, keep playing until you reach the marking **D. 𝄋. al Coda**—this basically means go back to the 𝄋 until you reach the **To Coda ⊕** marking, and then go to the **Coda**.

6 Skip back to letter A and play through that repeated section again until you reach the **To Coda ⊕** marking.

7 Then go to **⊕ Coda** and play through that section until the end.

Now try playing along with **Track 43**.

Tip

1 Make sure all the chords sound cleanly—no buzzes!

2 Play in time, with the chords on the beat. Don't worry about playing a continuous rhythm right away. Just get comfortable with the changes, and introduce more strumming as you gain confidence.

Changin' Time

◻ = downstroke

∨ = upstroke

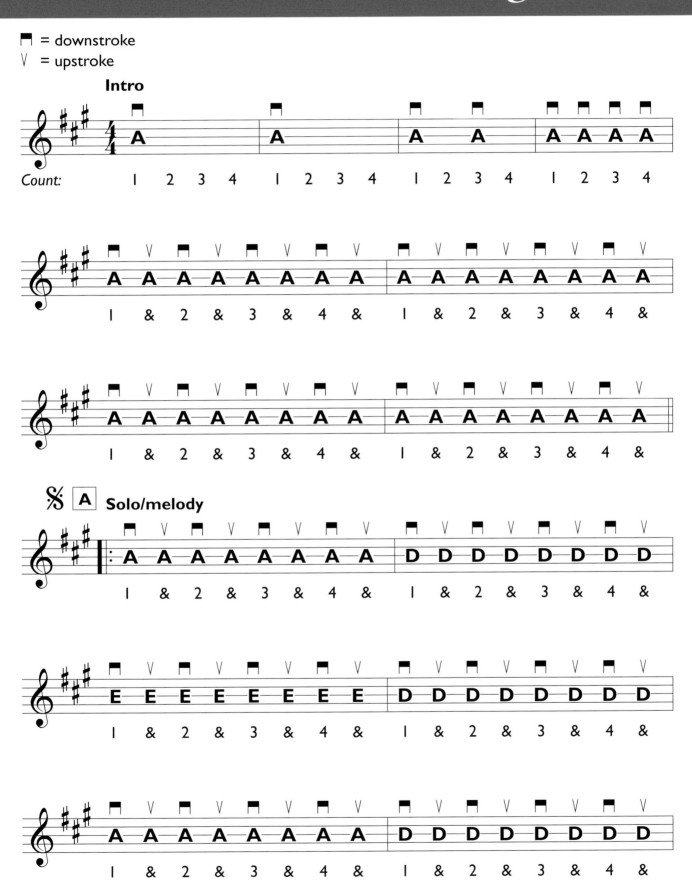

Changin' Time

1st & 2nd endings: play through the bars under the "1," then skip back to A
On the second pass, leave out the bars under "1," and go directly to the bars under "2."

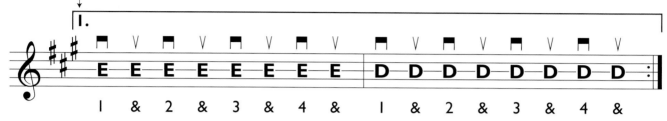

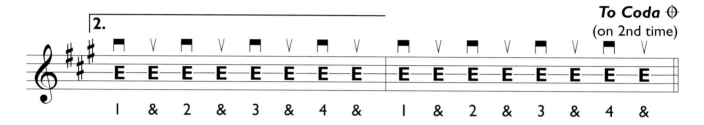

Changin' Time

Skip back to the Sign (%) at **A** and play through the 1st & 2nd endings.
Then, at To Coda ⊕ , skip ahead to the Coda below to finish the song.

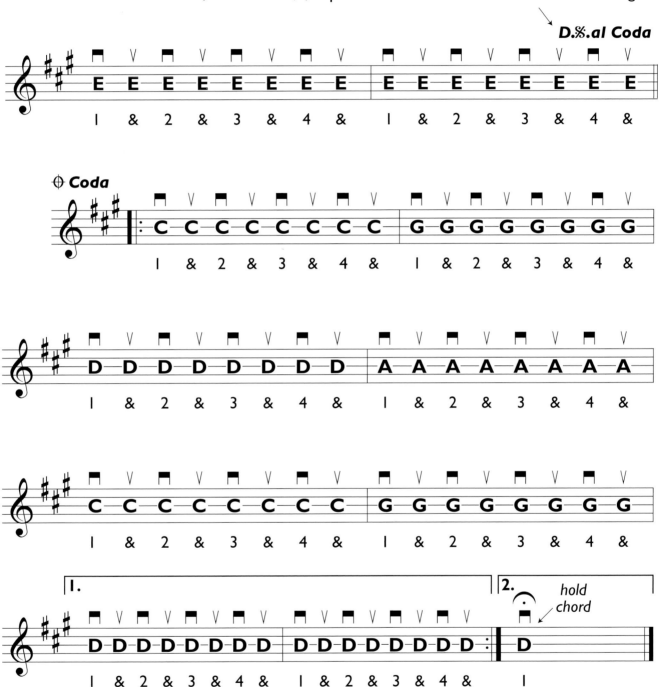

Some other chords

Here are some other essential chord shapes:

Remember that not all chords use all six strings—so watch which strings you hit!

Track 44

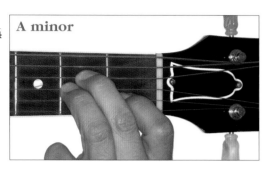

A minor

Don't strike the 6th string!

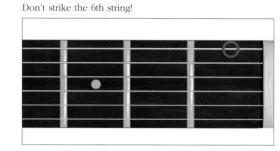

Track 45

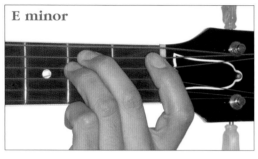

E minor

Track 46

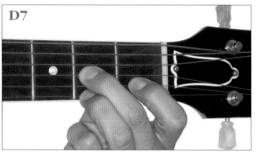

D7

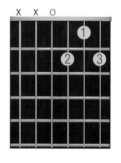

Don't strike the 5th and 6th strings!

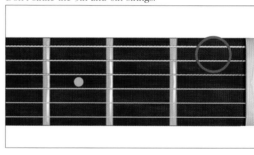

Track 47

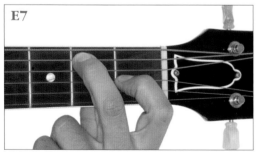

E7

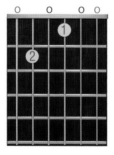

Track 48

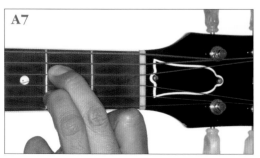

A7

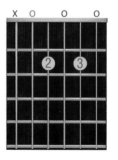

Don't strike the 6th string!

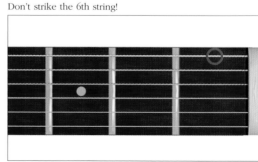

Now that you're comfortable with the world of chords, let's finish with a simple guitar melody that you can play along with the song you've just learned.

Introduction to TAB

Most guitar music uses a system called "tablature" (TAB) which tells you where to put your fingers when playing the single notes of a melody.

To play the simple melody of the song, let's briefly look at the TAB system.

1 Don't concern yourself with the music notation for now, concentrate on the TAB information. TAB is always written under the melody of the song.

2 The six horizontal lines of the TAB represent the six strings of your guitar; the bottom line represents the lowest (thickest) string, and the top line represents the highest (thinnest) string.

3 The numbers on those horizontal lines indicate the frets at which you should place your fingers.

The note D

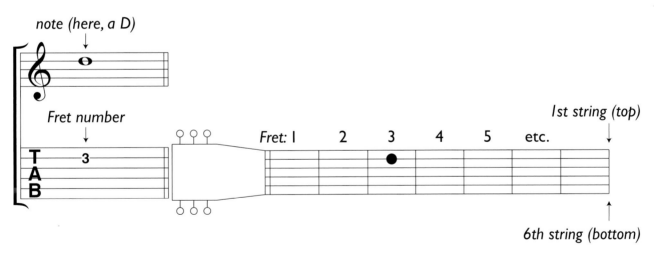

note (here, a D)

Fret number

1st string (top)

Fret: 1   2   3   4   5   etc.

6th string (bottom)

In the above example, the note is a D and is found at the 3rd fret of the 2nd string. You place your left-hand finger just behind the 3rd fret on the 2nd string.

Tip

Open strings are designated as 0 on the TAB line— don't fret the string, just play it open.

Adding a melody

Now you're ready to add the melody to "Changin' Time." Listen to **Track 42** to hear how this sounds. Practice it really slowly at first, concentrating on counting steadily. Once you're confident of the sequence of notes, build up the speed gradually until you can play along with **Track 43**.

There's no melody in the Intro so you'll have to count really carefully in order to come in in the right place. Listen to **Track 42** again until you're completely familiar with the song—then you'll be able to feel when it's the right time to start playing the melody.

After you've repeated the Solo/melody section, there's no melody until you reach the "D.S. al Coda" instruction, which then returns you to letter A.

Finally, there's a slightly modified form of the tune in the Coda, which will take you through to the end of the song.

Counting

Counting is one vital skill that all musicians need to master—especially if you ever want to play in a band.

In this song there are substantial gaps when there's no melody to play—continue counting 4 beats in a bar, but use the first beat of each bar as a count of how many bars you've rested for:

1 2 3 4, **2** 2 3 4, **3** 2 3 4, **4** 2 3 4 etc

Then you'll be ready for the moment when you have to start playing again.

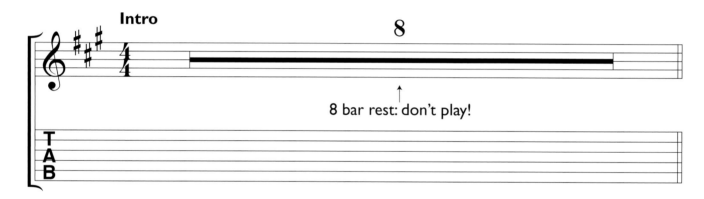

8 bar rest: don't play!

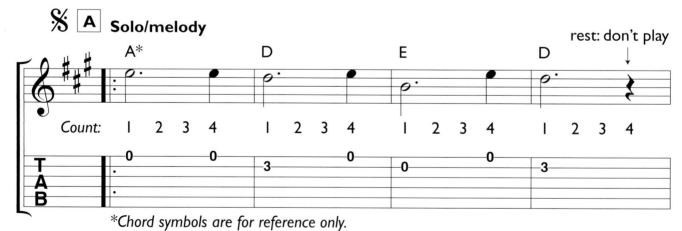

Chord symbols are for reference only.

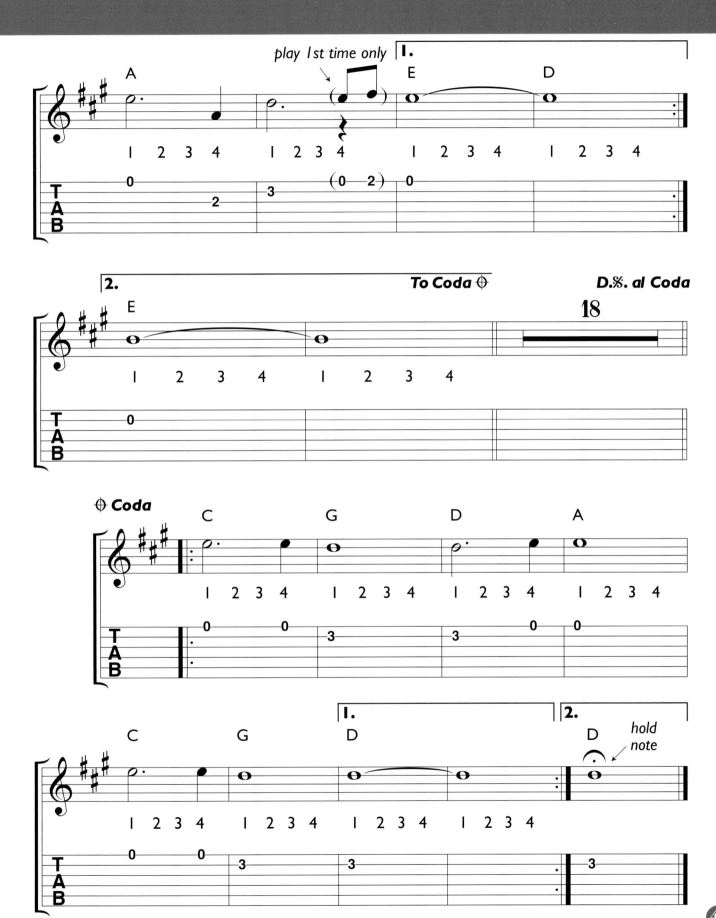

Congratulations!

I hope that you have enjoyed playing through *Part One* and that you will feel inspired to continue making music on your guitar in whichever style most interests you. Feel free to ask other players about their experience and techniques—they'll be able to pass on some useful tips and advice.

If you've made it this far, you've learned five of the most important guitar chords, and, more importantly, you have learned to change between them smoothly.

You've learned to strum in various patterns, using both up- and downstrokes, and you've developed your sense of rhythm so that you can play along with backing tracks.

Finally, you've put all those skills together and learned a complete song, with a solo guitar melody.

Armed with the skills you've learned in this book, you're now ready to tackle some classic songs. Check out some of the tunes listed below, and listen carefully to the guitar parts—most of them are simple chord changes using the chords introduced in this book.

Don't Look Back In Anger Oasis
Everybody Hurts R.E.M.
Everything Must Go Manic Street Preachers

Hey Joe Jimi Hendrix
How Soon Is Now? The Smiths
Jumping Jack Flash The Rolling Stones
Parklife Blur
Smells Like Teen Spirit Nirvana
Tears In Heaven Eric Clapton
Waterfall The Stone Roses
Wild Thing The Troggs
Won't Get Fooled Again The Who
Yesterday The Beatles

Eric Clapton

Keith Richards
The Rolling Stones

Peter Buck
R.E.M.

Kurt Cobain
Nirvana

Noel Gallagher
Oasis

iCanPlayMusic

Complete Guitar Course

PART TWO

Introduction

Welcome to *iCanPlayMusic: Guitar Part Two!*
If you're reading this, you've either completed all of the music in *Part One,* or you may already know a few chords and want to learn some of the more advanced techniques in this book.

CHECKLIST

By the end of *Part One,* you should have learned the following about the guitar:

Chords

You should know the chords A, D, E, G, and C by now. At the end of *Part One* you were introduced to Am, Em, D7, E7, and A7. You'll need these chords to play some of the examples in this book.

Holding the guitar

Whether you're using a strap or sitting down, you should have found a position in which the guitar is comfortable to play. The fretting hand should be able to reach any of the six strings easily, and the strumming hand should rest roughly near the soundhole or pickups.

Tuning up

Track 1

There are three ways to tune up:

- Using a reference, such as pitch pipes, tuning fork, CD, or piano;

- Tuning the guitar to itself (this is explained as "relative tuning" in *Part One);*

- Using an electronic tuner.

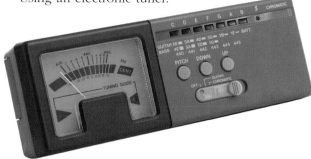

Strumming

By now you should be able to play alternating upstrokes and downstrokes with the strumming hand, and be familiar with the symbols for downstrokes (⊓) and upstrokes (∨).

By the time you've worked through all of the musical examples in this book, you'll be a more advanced rhythm guitar player, you'll have learned the basics of guitar solo techniques, and you'll have three complete pieces of music to play. Below is a list of everything you're going to learn.

Rhythm strumming

In this section, you'll learn how to make your rhythm parts sound more interesting and musical by using a combination of upstrokes and downstrokes with the pick.

Specialist techniques

Here, you'll be introduced to the techniques that professional guitarists use in their solos, including hammer-ons, pull-offs, and bends.

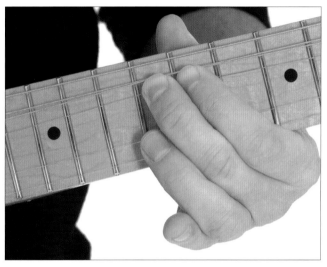

Lead guitar basics

Starting with a simple melody, you'll learn how to build up a lead guitar part, including picking techniques on electric or acoustic guitar, and how to make all the notes sound clearly.

Improvising your first solo

Who says you have to copy everything from books? This section will get you started on the mystic art of making up your own guitar solos.

New chords

This book introduces three new chord shapes, and helps you to learn the extra five from the end of *Part One*. At the end of the book you'll also be introduced to eight new chords so you can take your rhythm playing further.

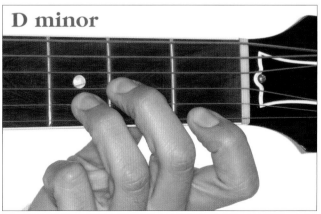

Chord reminder

In *Part One*, you learned the five major chords A, D, E, G, and C.

You may also have tried the five new chords shown here.

Note that these chords (two minors and three sevenths) have a more exotic and colorful sound than the simpler chords you've already learned.

You can hear these chords on CD **Tracks 44-48**.

Em

A minor

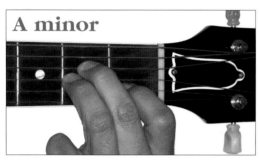

Don't strike the 6th string!

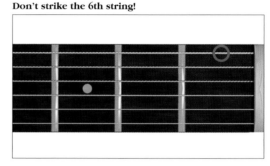

D7

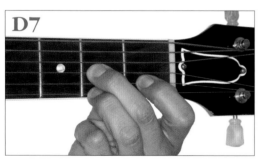

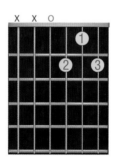

Don't strike the 5th and 6th strings!

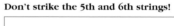

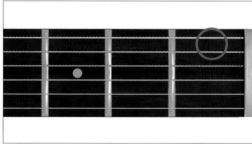

E7

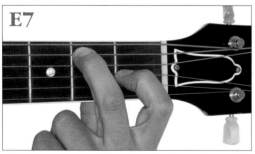

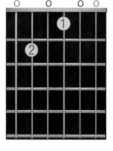

A7

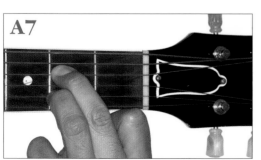

Don't strike the 6th string!

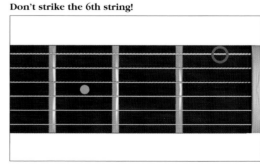

56

Shown here are three new chords to try out. You'll need the last one, B7, if you want to play rhythm guitar on the last piece in this book, "Booker's Blues."

Track 49

D minor

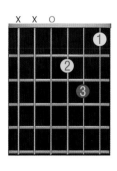

Don't strike the 5th and 6th strings!

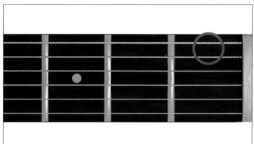

The chord of D minor (abbreviated Dm) often sounds good when played in the same song as Am and Em. Remember not to strike the two bass strings.

Track 50

C major 7

Don't strike the 6th string!

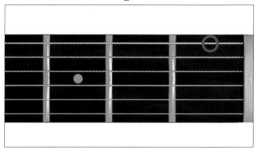

This is an example of a major seventh chord (abbreviated maj7). Try strumming it a few times, then changing to a Dm, and then changing back again. Instant jazz!

Track 51

B7

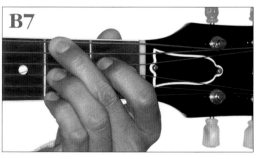

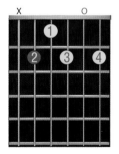

Don't strike the 6th string!

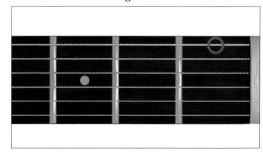

B seventh (abbreviated B7) is a good chord to use in blues music. Check out the example on page 86.

CHECKPOINT
WHAT YOU'VE ACHIEVED SO FAR...

You can now:
- Play the chords of Am, Em, D7, E7, and A7
- Play the new chords of Dm, Cmaj7, and B7

Rhythm guitar

DUDUDUDU strumming

In *Part One*, you learned a simple down-and-up strumming pattern.

Let's look at that technique in detail.

The example below uses a single A minor chord, and an even up and down strumming pattern, as you practiced in *Part One*. You can hear this example on CD **Track 52**. Note that the upstrokes and downstrokes are even in timing and in loudness.

This will take a good deal of practice to get exactly right.

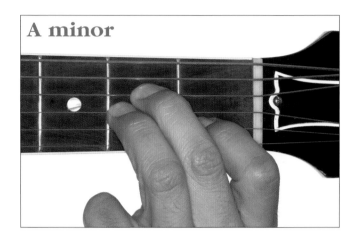

A minor

D	U	D	U	D	U	D	U
Am	Am	Am	Am	Am	Am	Am	Am

Count: 1 & 2 & 3 & 4 & etc.

Rhythm guitar tips

• Make sure your strumming hand is relaxed and you're not holding the pick too tightly

• Strum over the soundhole or pickups—not too near the bridge

• Aim for an even motion so that every upstroke lasts as long as every downstroke

• Start slowly and build up to speed—this will help to develop rhythmic accuracy

• Try tapping your foot with every downstroke—this will help to keep you in time.

• Don't strum too hard—this will make it more difficult to stay in rhythm, and can make the strings sound out of tune.

Once you've managed an even strumming technique, the next step is to develop a rhythmic pattern to make your chord accompaniments sound more interesting. Professional guitarists rarely play all of the down- and upstrokes—they usually leave gaps in their strumming for a rhythmic effect.

The next example leaves out two of the strums from our DUDUDUDU pattern. If your hand is moving evenly, the act of leaving out some of the strums will actually create a musical rhythm.

D	U	D	U	(rest)	U	D	(rest)
⊓	V	⊓	V		V	⊓	

Am — Am — Am — Am ——————— Am — Am

Count: 1 & 2 & 3 & 4 & etc.

Try leaving out the third downstroke and the final upstroke, which makes the pattern DUDU UD.

Note that you still have to move your hand across the strings to get ready for the next down- or upstroke.

The time you take to do this is what creates the rhythmic space in between the strums.

Repeat the pattern over and over while tapping your foot in time, and you'll soon get a feel for the technique. Listen to CD **Track 53** to check your timing.

CHECKPOINT

WHAT YOU'VE ACHIEVED SO FAR...

You can now:
- Play even upstrokes and downstrokes in time with the CD
- Play a rhythm guitar pattern using DUDU UD strumming

Now turn the page to use your strumming techniques in the track "Leavin' Space."

Leavin' Space

This piece of music will help you to practice three of the new chords—Am, Dm, and Em—and also to try out the strumming techniques we've covered so far.

It gets more difficult as the piece progresses because the chords get more and more rapid until, by the end, you're playing a rhythmic pattern and changing chords in time with the music.

Once you're confident playing along with the recording on **Track 54**, skip to the backing track on **Track 55,** which is the same piece of music without the rhythm guitar part. Remember, because the chords are the same on each one of the six repeats, you can try any strumming patterns you like as long as you play Am, Em, Dm, and Em.

Chords

Here's a quick reminder of the chords you'll be using for this piece:

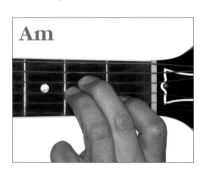

The next page shows the rhythm guitar chord chart for "Leavin' Space." Symbols have been used to show you the pattern of downstrokes and upstrokes.

The numbers underneath represent the beats you should count while playing. Four clicks at the beginning of **Track 54** will give you the count speed.

"Leavin' Space" rhythm guitar part

Note: the chords are the same each time around. Only the strumming hand changes.

1 After the four clicks, strum each chord once using downstrokes—Am, Em, Dm, Em. Use a single strum for each chord, and count for eight beats before you change to the next one.

2 Next, play the chords in the same order, but this time strum each one twice, and count four beats per strum.

3 Getting more difficult now. This time each chord is strummed four times, and you count two beats for each strum.

4 Now there's a strum on every beat, so each chord is strummed with a downstroke eight times before you change to the next one.

5 This time around, the acoustic rhythm guitar plays straight upstrokes and downstrokes. Count one-and-two-and-three-and-four while you play the regular strumming pattern we looked at (see page 58).

6 Now use the DUDU UD pattern (see page 59) while you change chords every eight beats. You've now added rhythm to the rest of the band's arrangement.

Outro Finish on a single ringing chord of A minor in time with the drummer's crash cymbal.

Leavin' Space

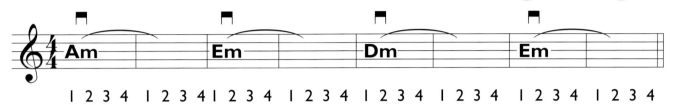

1 2 3 4 | 1 2 3 4 | 1 2 3 4 | 1 2 3 4 | 1 2 3 4 | 1 2 3 4 | 1 2 3 4 | 1 2 3 4

1 2 3 4 etc.

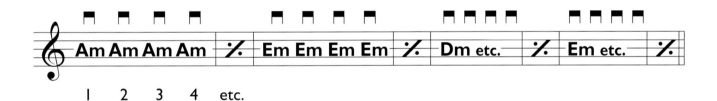

1 2 3 4 etc.

1 2 3 4 etc.

1 2 3 4 etc.

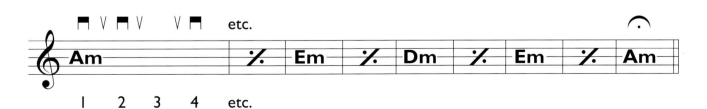

1 2 3 4 etc.

61

How to read guitar music

In the rest of the book, we'll be looking at fingerstyle and lead guitar playing. To do this you'll need a basic knowledge of guitar notation, so that you can see exactly what notes to play, and understand about rhythmic timing. Don't worry if it seems daunting at first—remember that all the examples are on the CD, so you should find the guitar music easier to read while the example is playing.

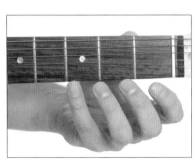 

Pluck the first string "open," *i.e.* without fretting a note…

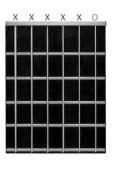

Now press the third fret on the second string and pluck that note…

Finally, press the first fret and pluck that note.

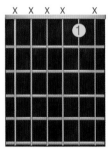

Three Blind Mice
All of the above information can be shown in tab like this.

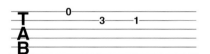

Using tab for chords
To notate chords, we simply stack the tab numbers on top of each other to show that all the notes are strummed at the same time. Here's a chord of Em shown in tab.

Em

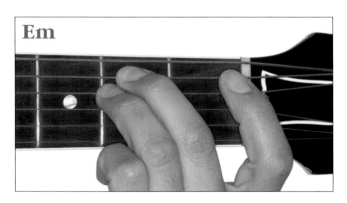

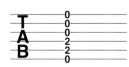

Am

To show how easy tab is to use, here's a version of every chord you've learned so far in *Part Two*, with the tablature shown under the photo.

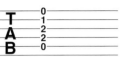

```
T --0--
A --1--
  --2--
  --2--
B --0--
```

Dm

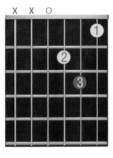

```
T --1--
A --3--
  --2--
  --0--
B
```

D7

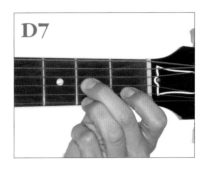

```
T --2--
A --1--
  --2--
  --0--
B
```

E7

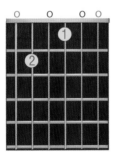

```
T --0--
A --0--
  --1--
  --0--
B --2--
  --0--
```

A7

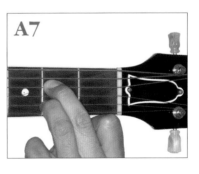

```
T --0--
A --2--
  --0--
  --2--
B --0--
```

B7

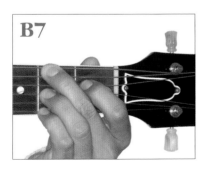

```
T --2--
A --0--
  --2--
  --1--
B --2--
```

Cmaj7

```
T --0--
A --0--
  --0--
  --3--
B
```

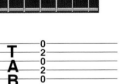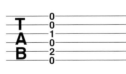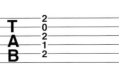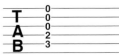

Fingerstyle guitar

In this section, we're going to explore the techniques and sound of fingerstyle guitar. This involves using the thumb and the first three fingers of the strumming or picking hand. The thumb covers the three thickest strings, and the three fingers cover one each of the thinnest strings.

The photo shows how your hand should be positioned to play fingerstyle.

Basic thumb and claw
Listen to CD **Track 56**, which is based on an A minor chord. In this example, the thumb is playing the open A string on its own, then the three fingers pluck the thinnest strings all together—this technique is called a *claw*.

Which way for the thumb?
Because the thumb has to cover all of the three thickest strings, we need to decide which one it should play for a given chord. Generally, fingerstyle players favor the *root note* of the chord. This is the thickest (or lowest) string in the chord that is not marked with an X in the fretbox.

In the case of an Am chord, this is the fifth string (open A). In the case of a D chord, for example, it would be the fourth string (open D). For an Em chord, it would be the sixth (thickest) string (open E). You get the idea.

▲ Fingerstyle hand position.

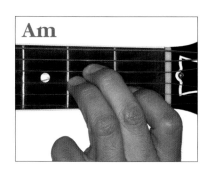

Am

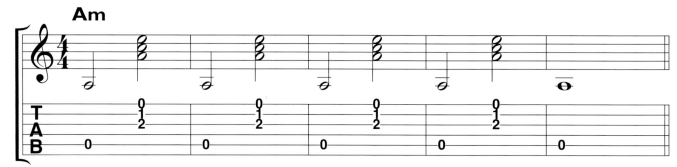

Am

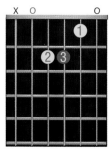

A minor facts:

I A minor is usually abbreviated to Am.

2 The A chord is named after its lowest note—the open A string (the 5th string).

3 Like most minor chords, A minor is characterized by a sad, melancholy sound.

64

Am

Listen to CD **Track 57**.

Here, the same thumb and claw pattern is played at double speed.

This is more difficult, and it's very tempting to strike the strings too hard (or miss them completely!) but persevere until you can achieve a gentle but fluent action, alternating between the single thumb bass note and the three-finger claw part.

Am

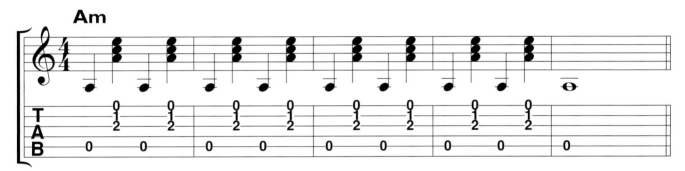

Tip

Getting lost?
Sometimes the picking hand fingers will tend to wander away from the strings, or you'll find yourself plucking the wrong strings by mistake.

Try anchoring your picking hand on the body of the guitar somewhere, for example by resting the heel of the hand gently on the bridge, or by pressing your little finger near the soundhole or pickups.

CHECKPOINT

WHAT YOU'VE ACHIEVED SO FAR...

You can now:
- Play an Am chord using thumb and claw techniques
- Play thumb and claw at speed with an even sound

More advanced picking

Now that you can control a basic claw, let's move on to something more adventurous.

CD **Track 58** uses a technique called an *arpeggio*. This means that you play a normal chord, but pluck the strings one by one instead of strumming.

Our first example uses a straight ascending arpeggio of Am.

Pluck the open A string with the thumb, then pluck the three thinnest strings one by one with your first, second and third fingers respectively. Start slowly and build up speed until the timing of the notes is absolutely even.

You may find that the fingers' notes sound louder than the thumb's at first—keep playing the example over and over until all the notes are at the same volume.

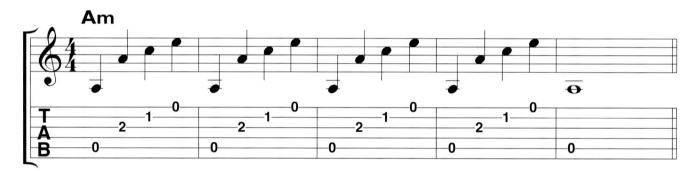

Am

x   o   o

Track 59
demonstration

In fingerstyle guitar, the thumb usually plays on the first beat of each bar (*i.e.*, on the count of "one").

The fingers' parts can be played in any order. Now that you can play a simple arpeggio, let's try to add some variation.

The next example uses a *staggered arpeggio*. This means that the fingers play the notes in a particular order, forming a fingerpicking pattern.

In this case, we're playing thumb, first finger, second finger, first finger, third finger, first finger, second finger, first finger. Try this really slowly at first and build up to an even tempo.

Am

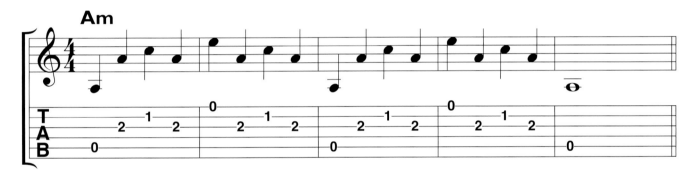

◀ Make sure your fingers stay close to the strings at all times—this way, the picking will require less effort, and your note choices will be more accurate.

CHECKPOINT
WHAT YOU'VE ACHIEVED SO FAR...

You can now:
- Play an ascending arpeggio
- Create a fingerpicking pattern

A new song Checking In

This country-rock piece will help you to put together all of the fingerpicking techniques you've learned so far.

On the recorded example, each technique is played one after the other, but you can use any of the techniques all of the way through if you wish as a way of practicing.

Checking In guitar part **Track 60**
Note: remember the chords of Am, G, D, and E are the same each time around. Only the picking hand changes.

1 Wait for six clicks and a slow drum beat, then play a slow thumb and claw (as on page 64) using the chords of Am, G, D, and E. Don't forget to change the thumb's bass note—it should be on the fifth string for the Am, the sixth (thickest) string for the G, the fourth string for the D, and back to the sixth for the E.

2 As before, but this time you should play a faster thumb and claw with the same chords (see page 65).

3 Play a slow ascending arpeggio (see page 66). Vary the thumb part for each chord as before, but keep the parts for the fingers of the picking hand the same.

4 As before, but play the ascending arpeggios at double speed. You may find this very difficult at first.

5 Now apply the variation part you learned on page 67 to each of the four chords at speed. This is even more difficult, but it sounds more interesting to your audience, so put in the effort to get it right!

6 Finally, let rip with big, wide strums using the DUDU UD strumming pattern (see page 59). Strum with the fingernails and thumb, or if you prefer, have a pick handy, ready to pick up just in time to start strumming. Don't forget—you should avoid strumming any strings marked with an X in the fretbox.

Outro Finish on a single, ringing chord of A minor in time with the drummer's crash cymbal.

Chord pattern
The song uses only four chords – Am, G, D, and E. These are played for two bars each (a count of eight fast beats per chord). To make the timing easier to follow, the song starts with six clicks, then a slow drum beat before your guitar part begins.

Track 60
demonstration

Track 61
backing track

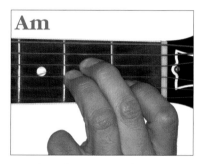
Am

Try this alternate G fingering:

G

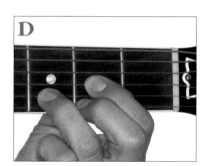
D

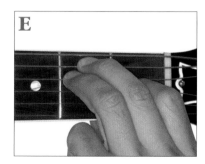
E

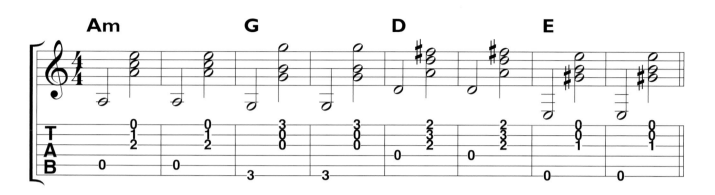

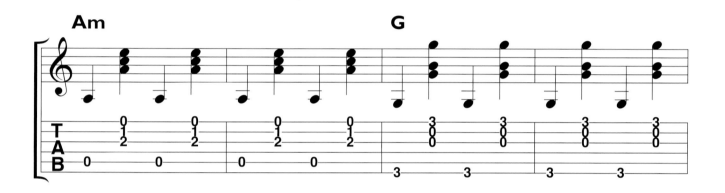

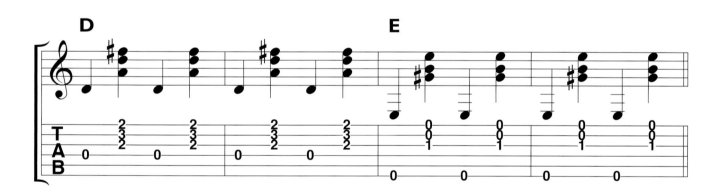

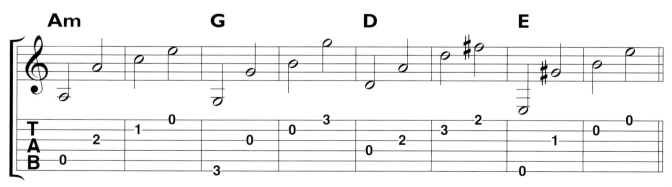

Checking In

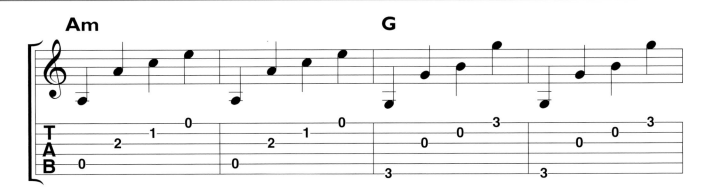

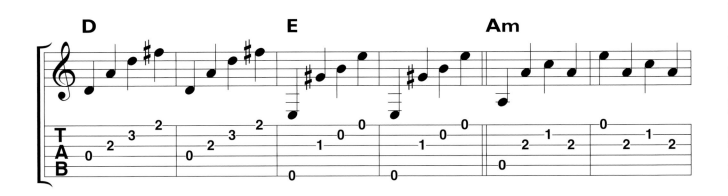

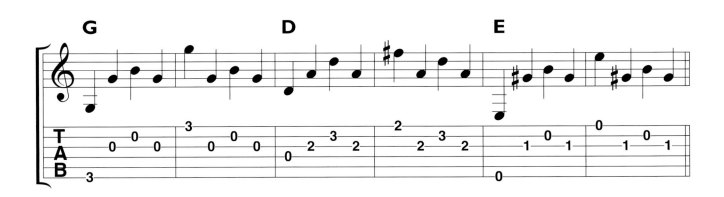

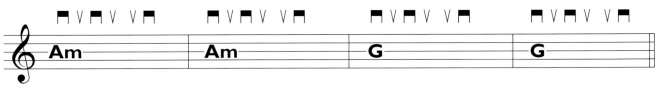

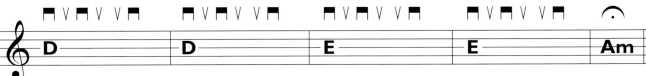

In this section, you're going to learn the basics of lead guitar. This is when the guitar plays single notes instead of chords.

Lead guitar tips

• Don't push the strings up or down unintentionally. This will bend the notes out of tune.

• Don't hold the pick too firmly or you'll be too tense to pluck the strings accurately.

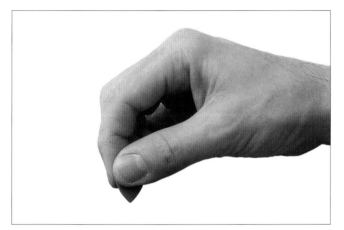

• Do play at a quiet volume (electric guitarists) until you have mastered each technique. A loud guitar amp is not pleasant to listen to if you're hitting wrong notes!

• If you're getting fret buzz from a note, move your fretting finger closer to the next fret to clean up the sound.

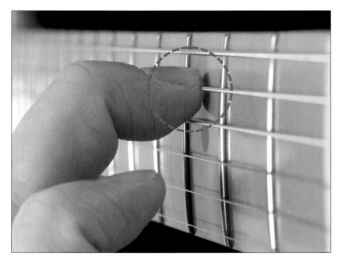

• Make sure your fretting hand has short fingernails —this will make fretted notes easier to hold.

• Do make sure you only play one string at a time. Lead guitar parts are usually played on an electric guitar, but can easily be played on acoustic if you prefer.

• Don't tense the forearm of your picking hand. A relaxed picking hand is the key to accurate picking.

• A good lead player uses a combination of up-strokes and downstrokes to aid speed.

• Keep the pick close to the strings, even when you're not playing a note.

• It may help accuracy if you anchor your hand somewhere on the body. Many players like to rest on their little finger, like this:

Fretting notes

Good lead guitar players usually observe the *one-finger-per-fret rule*.

This means that when you change frets, you don't move your whole fretting hand, but use a different finger for each fret, as shown in the photo below.

In this book, all of the lead guitar examples use the first finger at the first fret, the second finger at the second fret, and so on. This rule should be applied on every string.

Although this sounds obvious, you'll probably find that you tend to favor the first and third fingers of the fretting hand, because these are naturally stronger.

Try to train the second and fourth fingers to be equally strong by observing one-finger-per-fret whenever you practice.

When you're playing lead guitar, use one finger per fret whenever possible to get used to the technique and develop fluency.

For example, if you see a number 2 in the tab notation, use your 2nd finger at the 2nd fret.

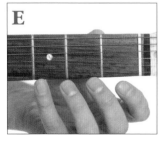

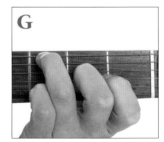

When you start playing lead guitar, you'll find that it's quite a challenge to move smoothly between notes.

Some notes will buzz, or may not sound at all, and you may find that strings will make an unintentional sound when you lift your fingers off.

On this page, I've included some hints and tips to help your lead guitar notes flow smoothly.

Smoother lead playing

• When you move from an open note to a fretted note, press the string onto the fingerboard fractionally before you pluck the string.

• When you move from a fretted note to a higher sounding fretted note (*e.g.*, 1st to 3rd fret), move to the higher sounding note before you take off the finger playing the lower sounding note

• When you move from a fretted note to a lower sounding fretted note (*e.g.*, 3rd to 1st fret), fret the lower sounding note before you take off the finger playing the higher sounding note.

• Practice moving between notes slowly and smoothly. If you get fret buzz, slow down and fret the strings more firmly, building up speed gradually as your fingers get used to the exercise.

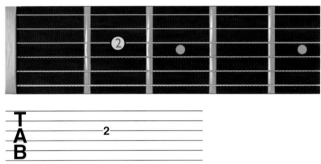

Warm-up exercise
Try the example shown here over and over until you can achieve a clean sound for each fretted note.

This is an excellent warm-up exercise before you start a practice session.

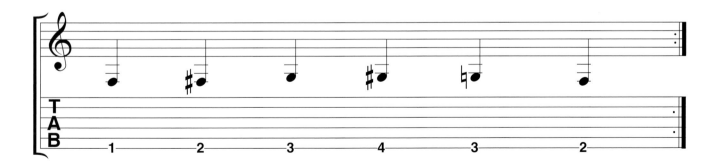

Let's play the blues!

Now you can use the techniques you've learned to play a classic electric blues lead guitar part. Over the next few pages, you can develop your lead guitar skills one at a time, and play a short piece of music for each. Each technique features a recorded example followed by a short backing track. When you've mastered all five techniques, you can put them all together and play the full song on **Track 70**.

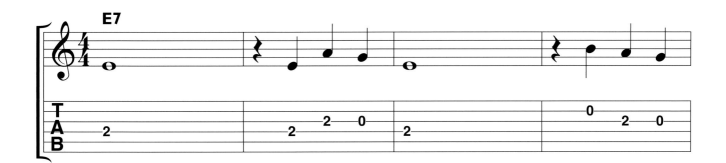

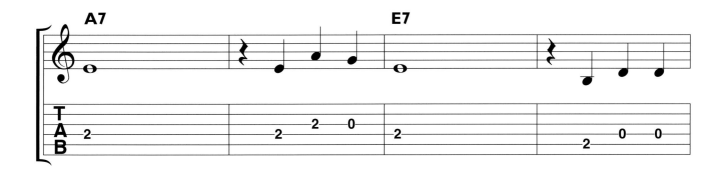

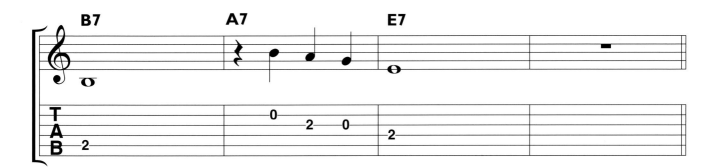

This is the simplest version of "Booker's Blues." Play each note using a downward picking motion with pick or fingers.

Track 62 "Booker's Blues" with picked notes

Track 63 backing track

CHECKPOINT

WHAT YOU'VE ACHIEVED SO FAR...

You can now:
- Pick lead notes cleanly and accurately
- Play the first version of "Booker's Blues"

Specialist techniques

Now that you can play the basic blues with picked notes, let's take a look in detail at the specialist lead guitar techniques we're going to cover.

Each is introduced one at a time, ending with a complete 12-bar blues that uses all four.

Hammer-ons
Pick one note, then fret a higher note on the same string without picking it. The second note is slightly quieter than the first, but has a smoother sound.

Vibrato
Bend a note up very slightly, then release the bend, and repeat over and over. If you do this very rapidly, you'll create vibrato.

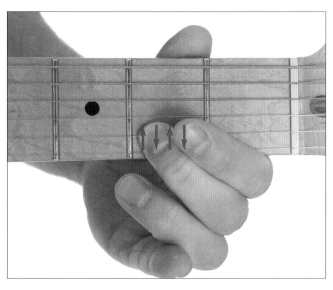

Bends
Fret a note, then push the string upward so that the note rises in pitch.

Pull-offs
The reverse of a hammer-on. Fret a note, then pull the string slightly with the fretting hand as you lift it off. You'll actually end up picking a note with the fretting hand.

Admit it—every guitarist wants to be able to play fast. In this section, we'll look at how you can increase fingerboard speed.

Speed tips

• When you're a beginner, it's quicker and easier to play from an open note to a fretted note, or vice versa, than to play two fretted notes. All of the examples in "Booker's Blues" use this idea throughout to make the lead part easier to play at speed.

• Where you see an open note followed by a fretted note on the same string, try using a hammer-on (see next page).

• Where you see a fretted note followed by an open note on the same string, try using a pull-off (see page 79).

• Use the one-finger-per-fret rule even if it feels unnatural at first—it will help you to play faster in the long term.

• Keep your thumb at the back of the neck rather than clamped around it.

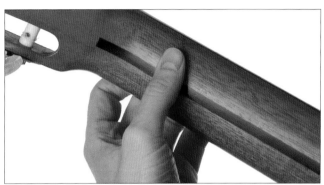

Hammer-ons

This speed technique is used heavily by rock and metal players, but you hear it crop up in virtually all styles of guitar playing, whether electric or acoustic.

Hammer-ons can only be played when the second note is higher in pitch than the first note.

How to play a hammer-on from an open string

1 Pluck an open note.

2 Let the note ring out clearly for a short time.

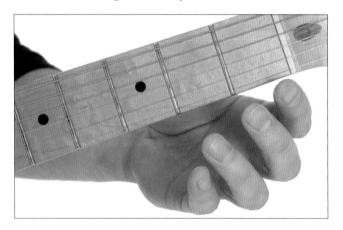

3 While the note rings on, fret any note on the same string as quickly and firmly as possible, using a "hammering" motion (the fretting finger should be at a right angle to the fingerboard).

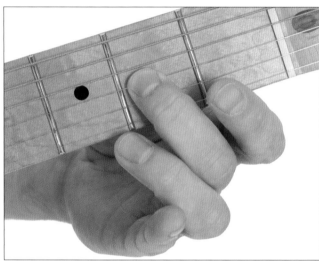

Hammer-on practice exercise
Play each open note then hammer on to the second fret with your second finger. Do this across each string in turn.

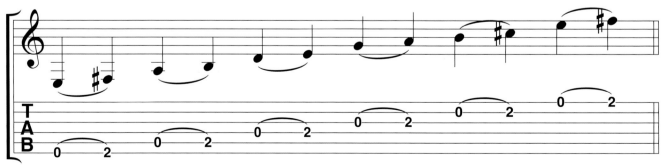

The opposite of a hammer-on is a pull-off. These can only be played when the second note is lower in pitch than the first note.

How to play a pull-off to an open string

1 Fret a note using one finger (*e.g.*, 2nd finger, 2nd fret, any string).

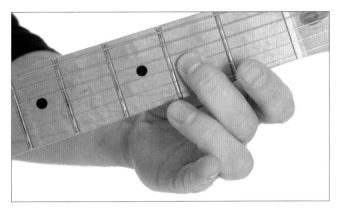

2 Pluck the note and let it ring out clearly for a short time.

3 While the note rings on, quickly pull the fretting finger off the string using a slight sideways motion— just enough to pluck the string as you take your finger off. The fretting finger should leave the fingerboard diagonally, and as you take your finger away, you should hear the lower note ring out.

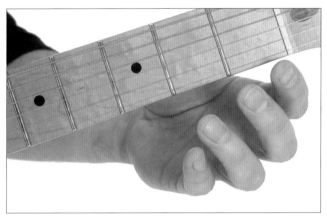

CHECKPOINT

WHAT YOU'VE ACHIEVED SO FAR...

You can now:
- Play a hammer-on from an open note
- Play a pull-off to an open note

Pull-off practice exercise
Start at the 2nd fret on the first (thinnest) string. Then pull off to the open note. Repeat this across the strings as shown until you get to the bass E string.

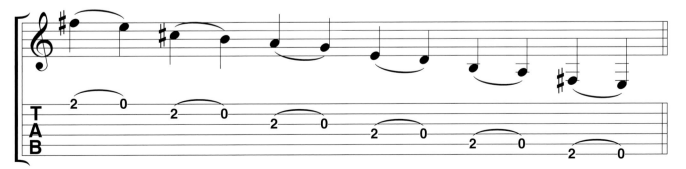

Booker's Blues – using hammer-ons

Here's a chance to use your new techniques in "Booker's Blues." First, we're looking at hammer-ons. There are fast hammer-ons in bars 1 and 3—work on getting these as fast as you can.

Track 64
demonstration

Track 65
backing track

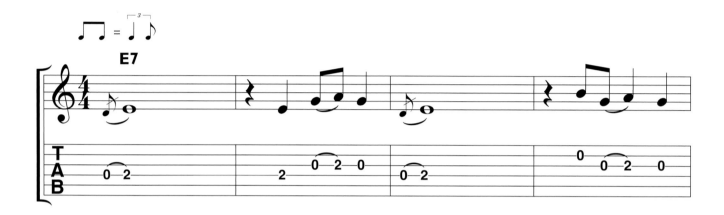

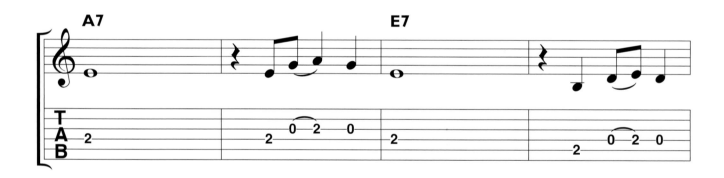

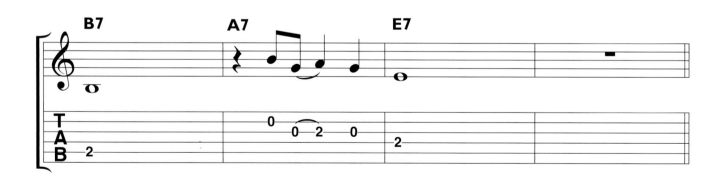

Booker's Blues – using pull-offs

This next variation of "Booker's Blues" is designed to help you practice your pull-offs. Watch out for bar 6—there are two in a row here. You might want to practice this bit slowly a few times before playing along with the CD.

Track 66
demonstration

Track 67
backing track

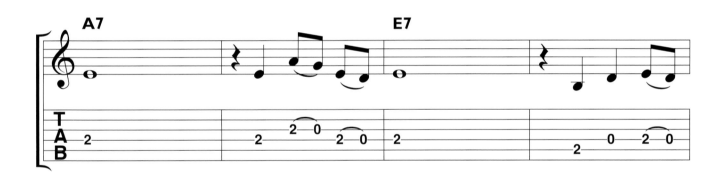

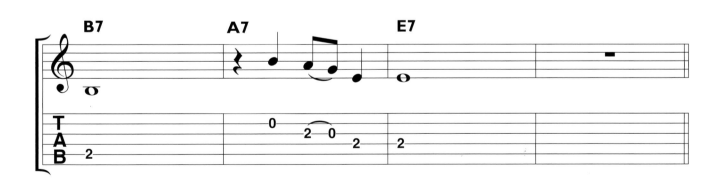

String bends

A string bend is achieved by pushing a string (usually upward) until it goes sharp (*i.e.*, it rises in pitch). In this book, all of the string bends should be played with the second finger, but as your technique develops, you should eventually be able to play a string bend with any of the fingers on your fretting hand.

Bends can be played on any guitar, but are much more difficult on an acoustic because the strings are generally thicker.

How to play an upward string bend

1 Fret any note (suggest you start with the second finger).

3 Push the fretting finger upward so that the note changes in pitch.

2 Pluck the string.

An upward string bend is notated like this:

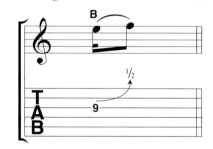

Tip

Support your bending finger with another finger.

How to play a downward string bend

1 Fret any note.

3 Pluck the string.

4 Release the tension so that the string returns to its normal pitch.

2 Push the fretting finger upward and hold the bent string.

A downward string bend (also known as a pre-bend) is notated like this:

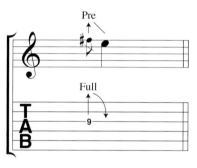

How to play an up-down bend

1 Fret any note.

2 Pluck the string.

3 Push the fretting finger upward so that the note changes in pitch.

4 Release the tension slightly so that the string returns to its normal pitch.

An up-down bend (also known as a bend-and-release) is notated like this:

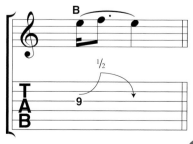

Vibrato

Vibrato (or *vib.* for short) is that professional sounding "wobble" that players put into a long, sustained lead note. There are two main types—rock vibrato and classical vibrato. Generally, rock vibrato is used on electric and steel-strung acoustic guitars. Classical vibrato is used on classical or flamenco guitars (*i.e.*, those that have three clear nylon strings).

How to play rock vibrato

1 Fret any note.

2 Pluck the string and hold the note to let it ring out.

3 Bend the note up very slightly...

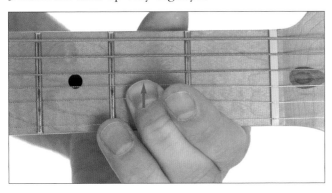

4 ...and release the bend again...

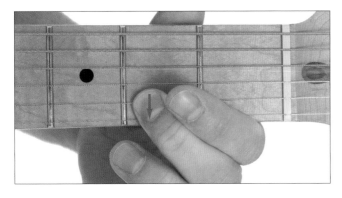

5 Repeat steps 3 and 4 over and over as fast as you can.

How to play classical vibrato

1 Fret any note.

2 Pluck the string and hold the note to let it ring out.

3 Holding the note as firmly as you can, pull the string very slightly towards the guitar body...

4 ...and pull it back again, towards the headstock...

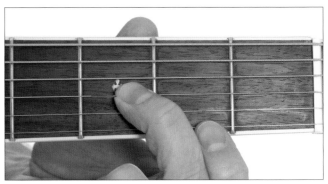

5 Wobble your hand backwards and forwards in this way as fast as you can while the note rings on.

However vibrato is played, it is always notated like this:

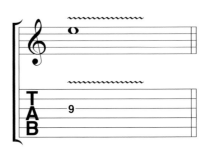

Now turn the page to use all of your new techniques in "Booker's Blues."

CHECKPOINT

WHAT YOU'VE ACHIEVED SO FAR...

You can now:
- Play an upward bend
- Play a downward bend
- Play an up-down bend
- Use vibrato

Booker's Blues – using vibrato

Now you can practice all the new techniques you've just learned in this next version of "Booker's Blues."

Track 68 demonstration   **Track 69** backing track

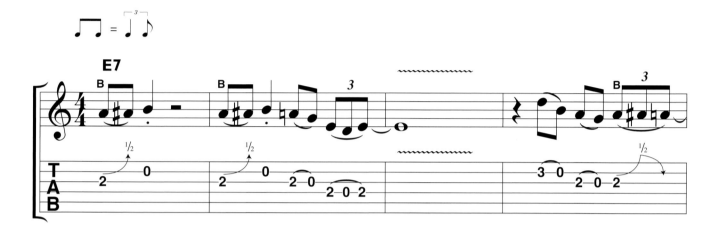

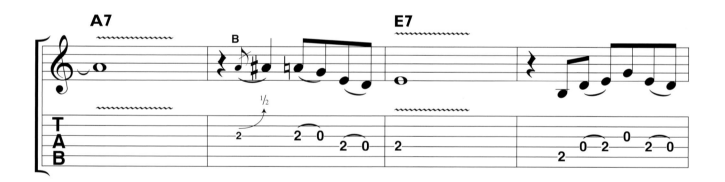

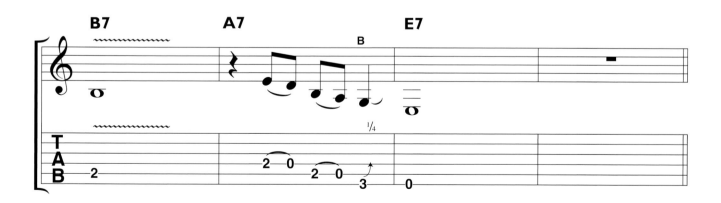

Putting it all together

It's now time to put it all together, to play the full-length version of "Booker's Blues."

Because the song is in a 12-bar blues format, you can repeat this chord sequence over and over.

Try playing four downstrokes per bar while you change chords.

You can choose to play rhythm or lead guitar over the backing track (CD **Track 71**).

The rhythm guitar part is shown below—why not make up your own strumming patterns?

E7

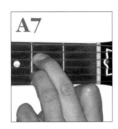

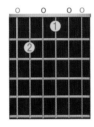
A7

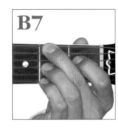
B7

| E7 | E7 | E7 | E7 |

| A7 | A7 | E7 | E7 |

| B7 | A7 | E7 | E7 |

Track 70
demonstration

Track 71
backing track

Booker's Blues

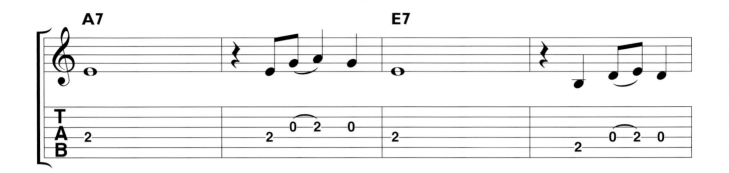

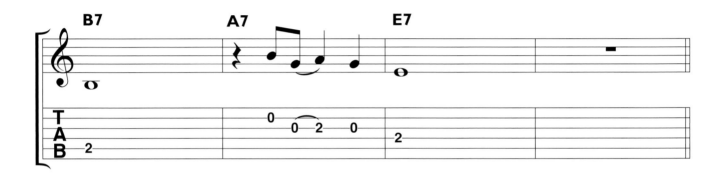

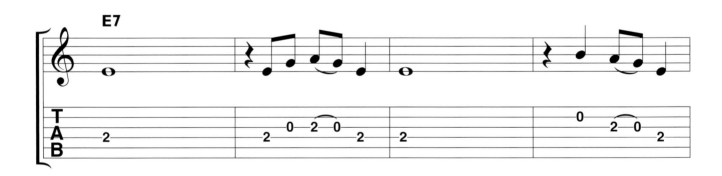

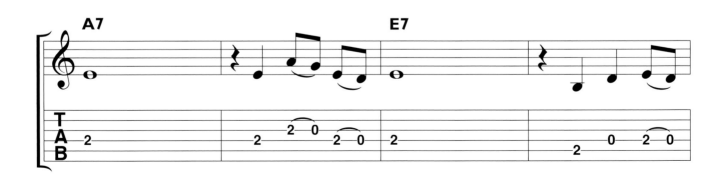

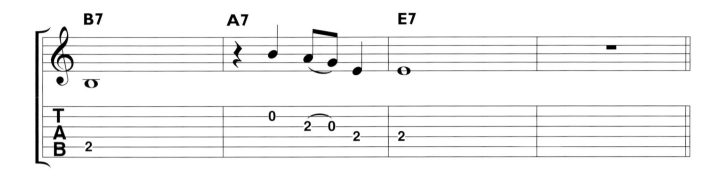

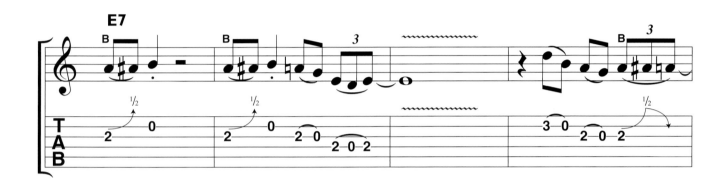

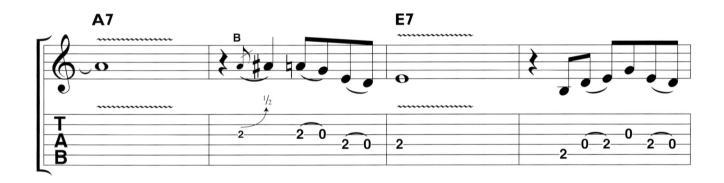

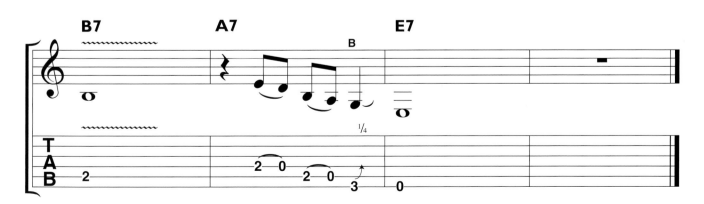

Congratulations!

If you've gotten this far and can play all of the pieces well, you've covered more than most beginners do in a whole year's worth of study.

LEARNING CHECKLIST

Rhythm strumming

You can now:

- use upstrokes and downstrokes accurately
- combine them to create rhythm patterns
- combine rhythm patterns with chord changes to play "Leavin' Space" and "Checking In"

Fingerstyle

You can play:

- thumb and claw at speed with chord changes
- arpeggiated chords using fingerpicking patterns

Lead guitar basics

You can now:

- pick notes accurately and fret them cleanly
- move smoothly from one note to the next
- use one-finger-per-fret technique
- play the first part of "Booker's Blues"

Specialist techniques

You can now:

- hammer on to an open note
- pull off to an open note
- play an upward bend
- play a downward bend
- use vibrato
- play all of "Booker's Blues" in full

The following few pages are designed to give you a few ideas about where to go next. I've introduced the idea of improvising, so you can try making up your own solos, and there are some more difficult chords to try out.

Improvising

If you choose your own notes to play in a lead part, this is improvising. On guitar, some improvisations are achieved by using a parent scale, the notes of which will sound good played over particular chords.

On this page, you'll see two of the most common improvising scales to get you started. Each can be played over one or more of the backing tracks on the CD.

Remember, when you're improvising, you can choose any note from the parent scale, and follow it with any other note, at any speed that suits you. Simply use your ears to tell you which combinations of notes sound good. As a famous rock guitarist once said, "It's a feel thing, man…"

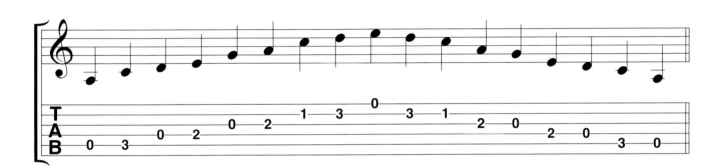

A minor pentatonic scale
Play any notes from this scale over the backing tracks for "Leavin' Space" or "Checking In" (CD **Track 55** and **Track 61**).

Am pentatonic scale Track 72

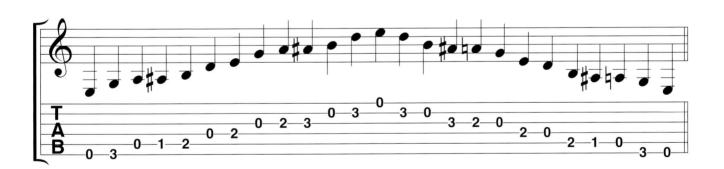

E blues scale
Play any notes from this scale over the backing track for "Booker's Blues" (CD **Track 71**).

E blues scale Track 73

New chords to try

Here are some further ideas for chords. Note that these all have more colorful, jazzy sounds than the basic major and minor chords you have used so far.

Track 74 **Em7**

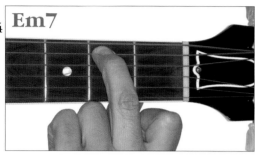

Track 75 **Dm7**

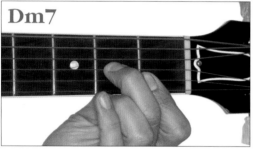
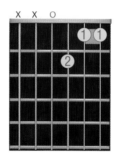

Don't strike the 5th and 6th strings!

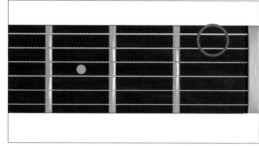

Track 76 **Gmaj7**

Track 77 **Dmaj7**

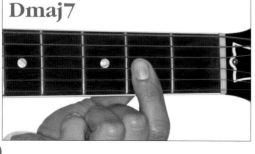

Don't strike the 5th and 6th strings!

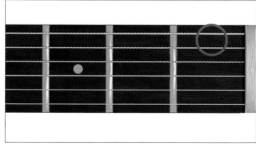

Bar chords

All of the chords on this page rely on a *bar* technique —i.e., flattening your first finger over all six strings.

Bar chords are the most versatile type of guitar chord, but they are also the most difficult, so expect to put in several weeks (or months!) of practice before you can play all of these cleanly.

When you can play a bar chord, try moving the whole chord shape up the neck by one or more frets.

This instantly gives you a different chord without having to learn a new shape. For example, if you move the chord of F up to the 2nd fret, you get the chord of F♯.

Track 78

F

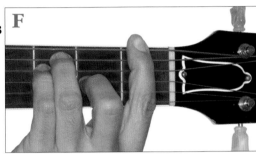
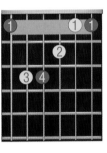

Track 79

Fm

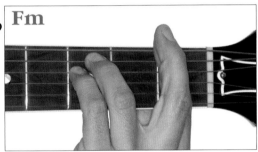

Track 80

B♭

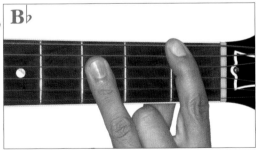

Don't strike the 6th string!

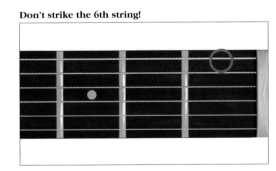

Track 81

B♭m

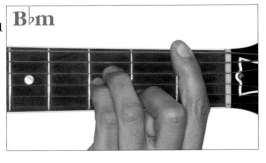

Don't strike the 6th string!

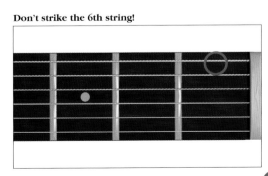

Gear guide

To play the examples in this book as they sound on the CD, you will need the following equipment:

EQUIPMENT CHECKLIST

- **Electric guitar**

The examples in this book can be played on any type of electric guitar regardless of its design. The two most common electric guitars are the Gibson Les Paul and the Fender Stratocaster. Many companies make cheaper copies of these guitars, which look and sound very similar to the authentic version.

- **Good quality guitar cord**

To check if your guitar cord is good quality, wobble it from side to side while it is plugged into the guitar and amplifier. If you hear a loud crackling sound you should replace the cord.

- **Amplifier**

Most amplifiers come with two guitar effects built in—*distortion/overdrive* and *reverb*. You can achieve distortion on many amplifiers by turning up the gain or drive control and turning down the master volume slightly. Other amplifiers have a special channel switch especially for distortion. Read the manual that came with your amplifier to learn how to achieve a distorted tone.

Reverb is a subtle echo-like effect. Most players find that they prefer their guitar sound with some reverb added to it. Try setting the control at about 50% and then turn it up or down until you get a reverb sound that you like.

All of the lead guitar sounds on the CD recordings use distortion and reverb only.

- **Effects**

If your amplifier doesn't have distortion or reverb (or even if it does), you may wish to use effects pedals to alter the basic guitar sound. The three most common effects are *distortion*, *reverb,* and *chorus*. If you use a distortion pedal with an amplifier, you usually get a better rock sound by using the pedal or the amp's distortion—but not both together. Some products feature many different effects all available from one unit—these are called *multi-FX*. Budget multi-FX units are usually a cheaper way of achieving different guitar sounds than buying individual effects pedals.

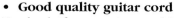

• Spare strings

If you break a string, you should replace all of the strings rather than just the broken one. This will ensure that your guitar maintains an even sound, and is easier to play.

• String cleaner

You should clean your strings every time you play, ideally at the end of each practice session.
Music shops will sell you a specialized string cleaner. Alternatively, just wipe the strings with a soft cloth.

• Capo

A capo lets you change the pitch of the guitar's open strings by clamping over the neck at a particular fret. Capos can be used on electric or acoustic guitars.

• Electronic tuner

Electronic tuners are a very quick way of tuning electric or acoustic guitars. Prices start at around $15.

• Guitar case

There are three types of guitar case. In ascending order of cost, these are:

Soft case—a bag that will protect your guitar from rain and dust, but not from hard knocks.

Gig bag—a padded bag with a shoulder strap. If you travel with your guitar regularly, this is the minimum level of protection it should have.

Hard case—this is the most expensive way of protecting your instrument. Most mid-priced and all expensive guitars come with a hard case as standard.

iCanPlayMusic

Complete Guitar Course

Introduction

The Chord Diagram

The chords are displayed as diagrams that represent the fingerboard of the guitar. There are six vertical lines representing the six strings of the guitar. Horizontal lines represent the frets. The strings are arranged with the high E (first, or thinnest) string to the right, and the low E (sixth, or thickest) to the left. The circles indicate at which fret the finger is to be placed and the number tells you which finger to use. At the top of the diagram there is a thick line indicating the nut of the guitar. Diagrams for chords up the neck just have a fret line at the top with a Roman numeral to the right to identify the first fret of the chord. Above the chord diagram you will occasionally see X's and O's. An X indicates that the string below it is either not played or damped; an O simply means the string is played as an open string. At the bottom of the diagram are the note names that make up the chord. This information can be helpful when making up lead licks or chord solos. A solid line tells you to bar the strings with the finger shown; that is, lay your finger flat across the indicated strings.

The fingerings in this book might be different from fingerings you have encountered in other chord books. They were chosen for their overall practicality in the majority of situations.

The Photo

The photo to right of each chord diagram shows you what your hand should look like on the guitar fingerboard. You will notice that the finger positions in some of the photos are a little to the right or left of the frame. This is done to show the particular chord form's proximity to either the twelfth fret or the nut of the guitar. This makes it easier to recognize the relative position on the fretboard at a glance.

Although the photos are a visual reference, all of the fingers in a given shot may not be in a proper playing position. We have sometimes moved unused fingers *out of the way,* to give you a better look at where the fretting fingers are placed. For instance, when playing the Em7b5 shown in the photograph below, your second and fourth fingers should not be tucked under the neck, but relaxed and extended upward over the fingerboard. Make sure your fingers are comfortable and that you are capable of moving them easily from one chord position to another.

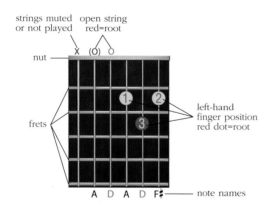

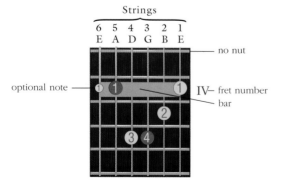

In order to talk about chord structure we need to discuss the foundation by which chords are formed—scales. There are a multitude of scales available to the musician, but we will explain only those that are most pertinent—the major, minor, and chromatic scales.

Major

| I | II | III | IV | V | VI | VII | VIII | VII | VI | V | IV | III | II | I |

Harmonic minor

| I | II | III | IV | V | VI | VII | VIII | VII | VI | V | IV | III | II | I |

Melodic minor

| I | II | III | IV | V | VI | VII | VIII | VII | VI | V | IV | III | II | I |

Chromatic

Scales are determined by the distribution of half steps and whole steps. For example, the major scale has half steps between scale steps three and four, and between seven and eight. The harmonic minor has half steps between scale steps two and three, five and six, and seven and eight. The melodic minor scale's ascending order finds half steps between scale steps two and three, and between seven and eight. Descending, the half steps fall between scale steps six and five, and between three and two; and a whole step is now in place between eight and seven.

It is common to refer to scale steps, or *degrees,* by Roman numerals as in the examples above and also by the following names:

I	Tonic
II	Supertonic
III	Mediant
IV	Subdominant
V	Dominant
VI	Submediant
VII	Leading tone

Intervals and chords

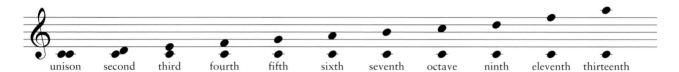

An interval is the distance between two notes. This is the basis for harmony (chords). The naming of intervals, as in the example below, is fairly standard, but you may encounter other terminology in various forms of musical literature.

| unison | second | third | fourth | fifth | sixth | seventh | octave | ninth | eleventh | thirteenth |

Chords are produced by combining two or more intervals, and the simplest of these combinations is a *triad*. A triad consists of three notes obtained by the superposition of two thirds. The notes are called the *root*, the *third*, and the *fifth*.

Inversions are produced by arranging the intervals of a chord in a different order. A triad that has the root as the bottom or lowest tone is said to be in *root position.* A triad with a third as the bottom or lowest tone is in *first inversion,* and a triad with a fifth as the bottom or lowest tone is in *second inversion.* As the chords become more complex—such as, sixths, sevenths, *etc.*—there will be more possible inversions.

root position   first inversion   second inversion

Note that when inverting more complex chords the inversion may actually become a completely different chord.

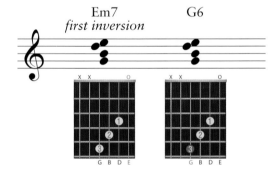

When a chord consists of a root, major third, and a perfect fifth it is known as a *major* triad. When the triad is altered by lowering the major third one half-step, it becomes a *minor* triad. The examples below are chords that have altered intervals.

C Chords

C major

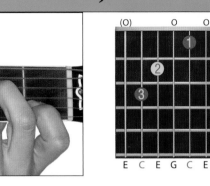

E C E G C E

C major

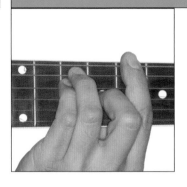

VIII

C G C E G C

Csus4

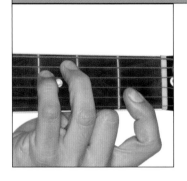

C F G C F

C6

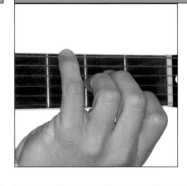

G E A C

C7

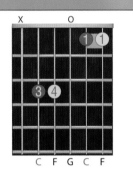

G C E B♭ C E

C°7

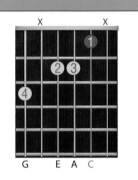

C G♭ B♭♭ E♭

C9

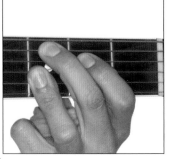

C E B♭ D G

C13

C E B♭ D A

Cmaj7

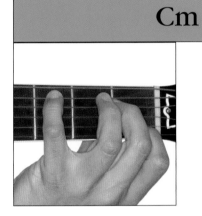

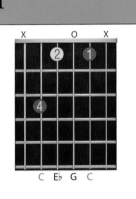

X   o o o

C E G B E

Cm7

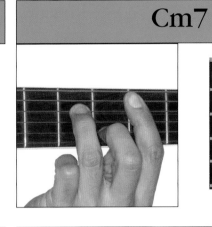

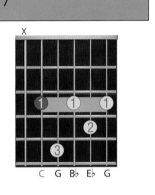

X

C G Bb Eb G

Cm

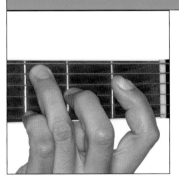

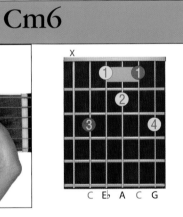

X   O   X

C Eb G C

Cm

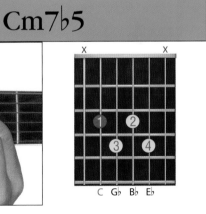

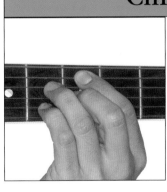

G C G C Eb G

Cm6

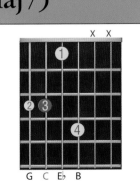

X

C Eb A C G

Cm7b5

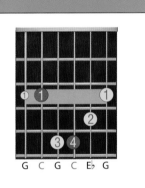

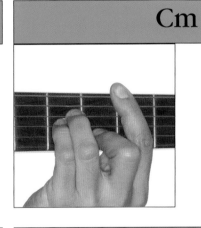

X   X

C Gb Bb Eb

Cm(maj7)

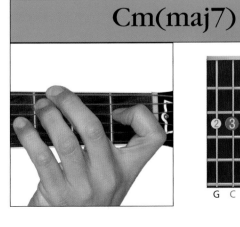

X X

G C Eb B

Cm11

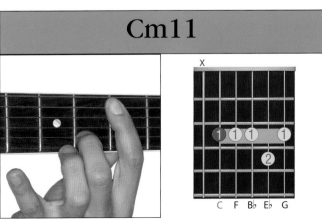

X

C F Bb Eb G

103

C♯ major

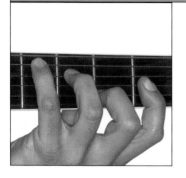
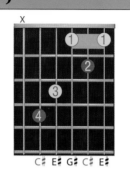

C♯ E♯ G♯ C♯ E♯

C♯ major

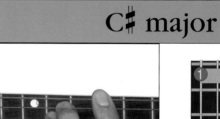
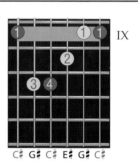

IX

C♯ G♯ C♯ E♯ G♯ C♯

C♯sus4

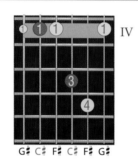

IV

G♯ C♯ F♯ C♯ F♯ G♯

C♯6

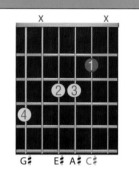

G♯ E♯ A♯ C♯

C♯7

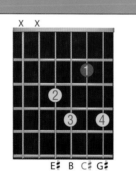

E♯ B C♯ G♯

C♯°7

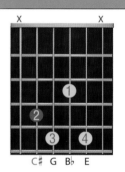

C♯ G B♭ E

C♯9

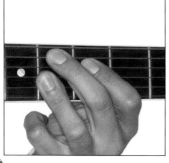
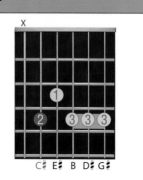

C♯ E♯ B D♯ G♯

C♯13

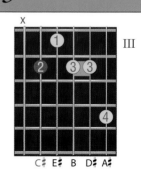

III

C♯ E♯ B D♯ A♯

C#maj7

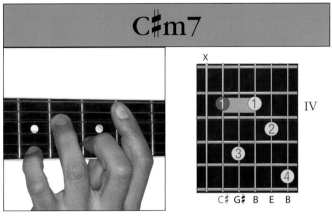

C# E# G# B# E#

C#m7

C# G# B E B

IV

C#m

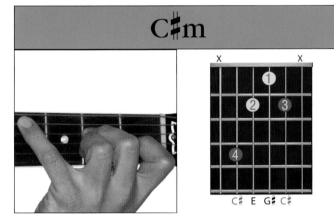

C# E G# C#

C#m

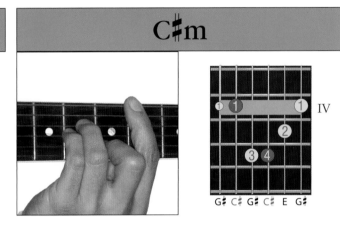

G# C# G# C# E G#

IV

C#m6

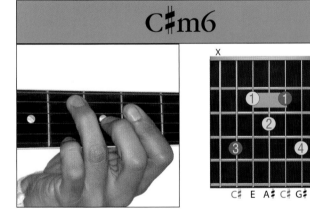

C# E A# C# G#

C#m7♭5

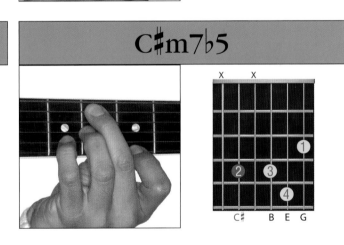

C# B E G

C#m(maj7)

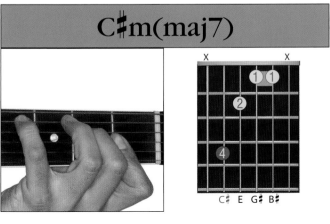

C# E G# B#

C#m11

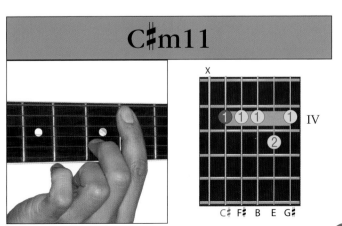

C# F# B E G#

IV

D Chords

 Track 5

D major

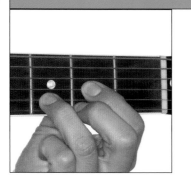 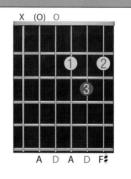

X (O) O

A D A D F#

D major

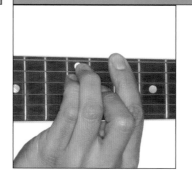 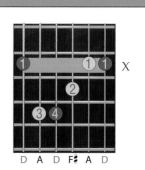

X

D A D F# A D

Dsus4

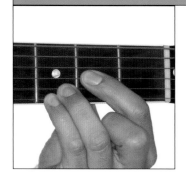 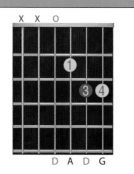

X X O

D A D G

D6

 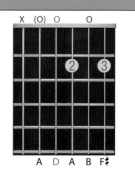

X (O) O O

A D A B F#

D7

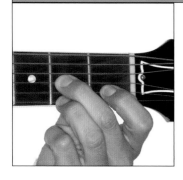 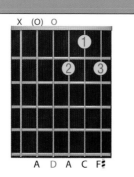

X (O) O

A D A C F#

D°7

 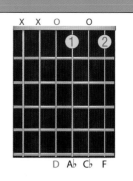

X X O O

D A♭ C♭ F

D9

 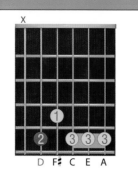

X

D F# C E A

D13

 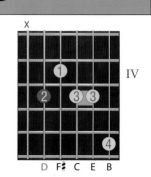

X

IV

D F# C E B

106

Dmaj7

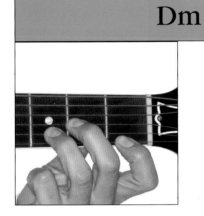

X (O) O

A D A C# F#

Dm7

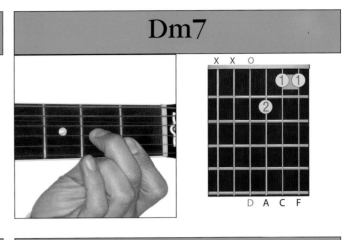

X X O

D A C F

Dm

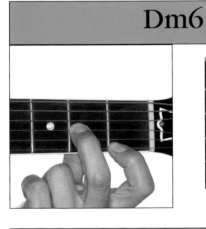

X (O) O

A D A D F

Dm

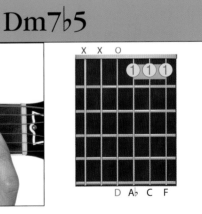

V

A D A D F A

Dm6

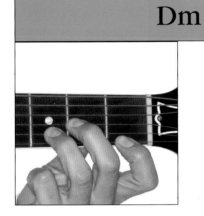

X X O O

D A B F

Dm7♭5

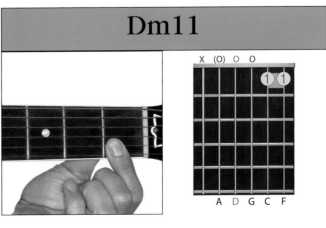

X X O

D A♭ C F

Dm(maj7)

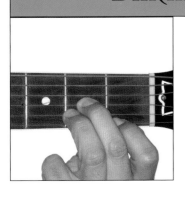

X X O

D A C# F

Dm11

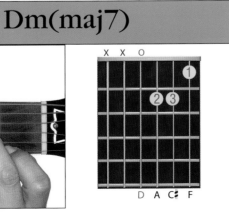

X (O) O O

A D G C F

107

Track 6

E♭ major

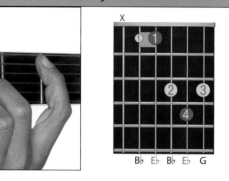

Bb Eb Bb Eb G

E♭ major

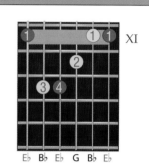
XI

Eb Bb Eb G Bb Eb

E♭sus4

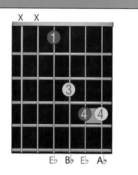

Eb Bb Eb Ab

E♭6

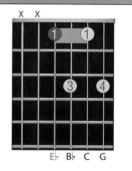

Eb Bb C G

E♭7

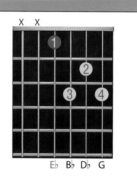

Eb Bb Db G

E♭°7

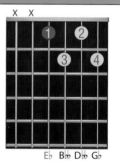

Eb Bbb Dbb Gb

E♭9

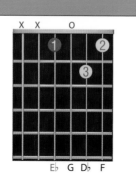

Eb G Db F

E♭13

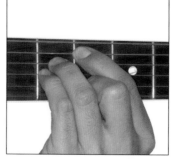

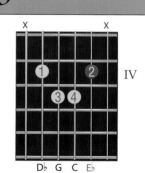
IV

Db G C Eb

Ebmaj7

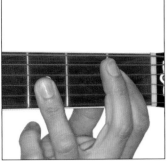

Eb Bb D G

Ebm7

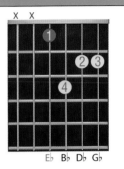

Eb Bb Db Gb

Ebm

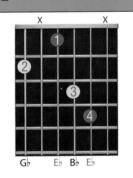

Gb Eb Bb Eb

Ebm

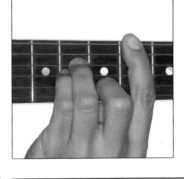
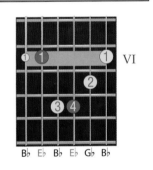

VI

Bb Eb Bb Eb Gb Bb

Ebm6

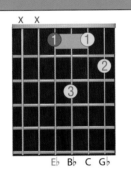

Eb Bb C Gb

Ebm7b5

Eb Bbb Db Gb

Ebm(maj7)

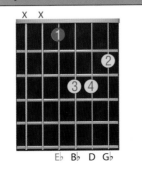

Eb Bb D Gb

Ebm11

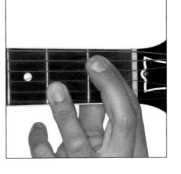
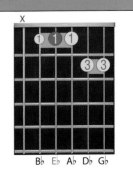

Bb Eb Ab Db Gb

109

E major

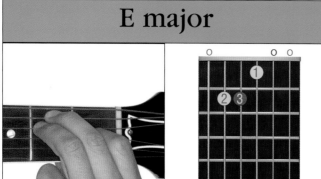

O   O   O

E B E G# B E

E major

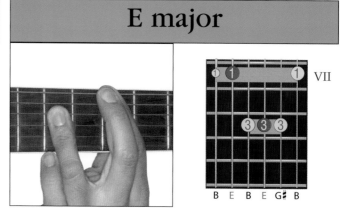

VII

B E B E G# B

Esus4

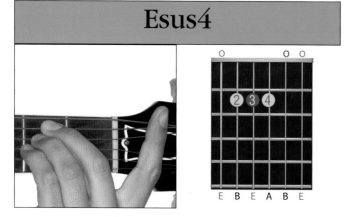

O   O   O

E B E A B E

E6

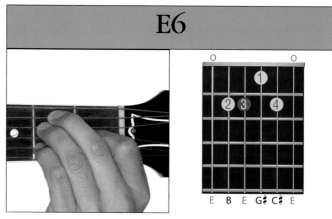

O   O

E B E G# C# E

E7

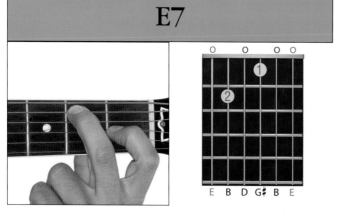

O   O   O O

E B D G# B E

E°7

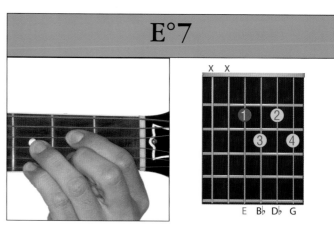

X   X

E B♭ D♭ G

E9

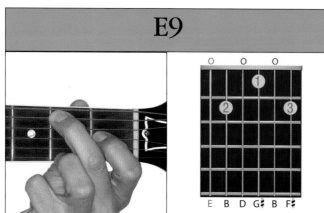

O   O   O

E B D G# B F#

E13

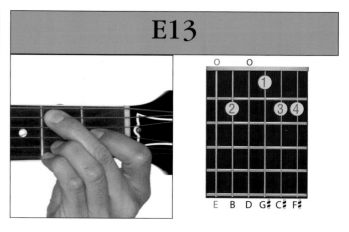

O   O

E B D G# C# F#

Emaj7

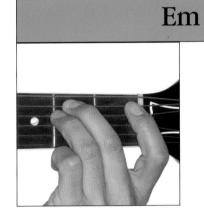

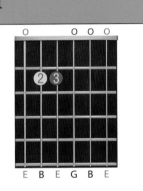

E B E G# D# E

Em7

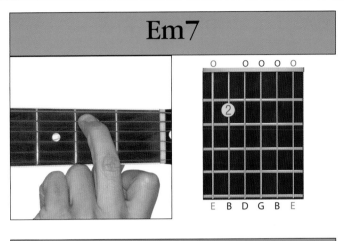

E B D G B E

Em

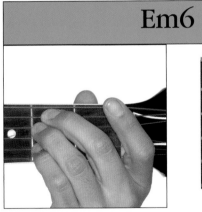

E B E G B E

Em

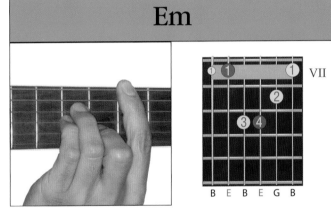

VII

B E B E G B

Em6

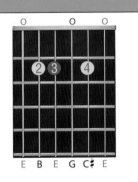

E B E G C# E

Em7♭5

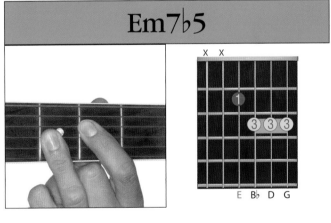

X X

E B♭ D G

Em(maj7)

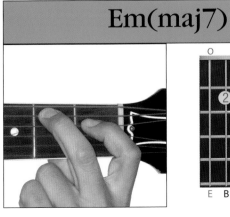

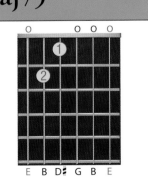

E B D# G B E

Em11

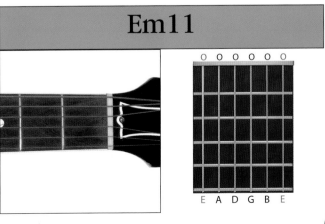

E A D G B E

111

F Chords

F major

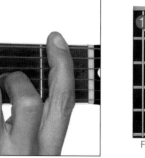
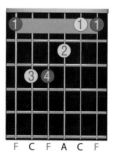

F C F A C F

F major

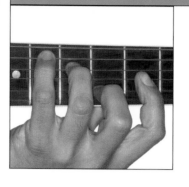
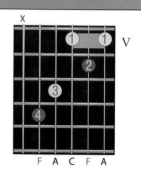

x

F A C F A

V

Fsus4

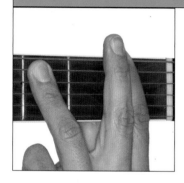
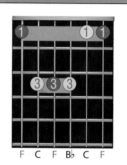

F C F Bb C F

F6

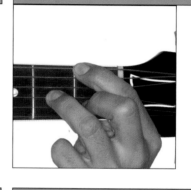
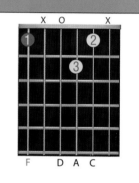

x o x

F D A C

F7

F C Eb A C F

F°7

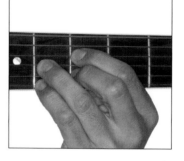
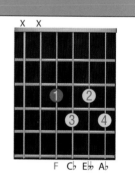

x x

F Cb Ebb Ab

F9

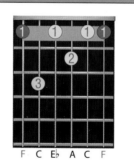

x x

F A Eb G

F13

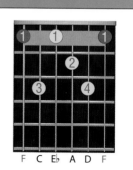
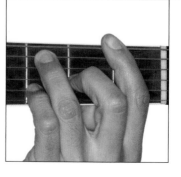

F C Eb A D F

Fmaj7

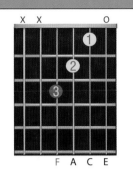

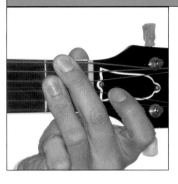

X X   O

F A C E

Fm7

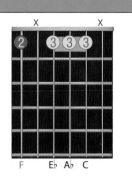

X   X

F Eb Ab C

Fm

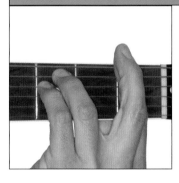

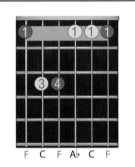

F C F Ab C F

Fm

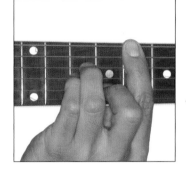

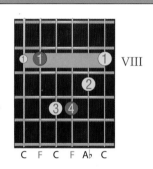

VIII

C F C F Ab C

Fm6

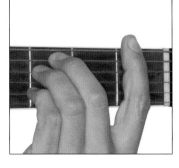

F C F Ab D F

Fm7b5

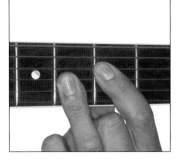

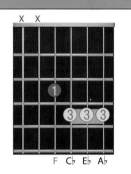

X X

F Cb Eb Ab

Fm(maj7)

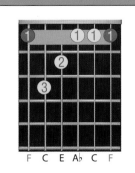

F C E Ab C F

Fm11

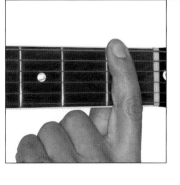

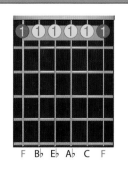

F Bb Eb Ab C F

Track 9

F♯ major

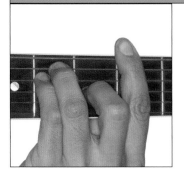
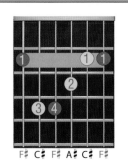

F# C# F# A# C# F#

F♯ major

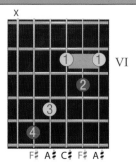

X

VI

F# A# C# F# A#

F♯sus4

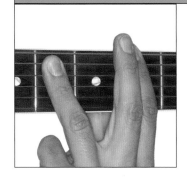
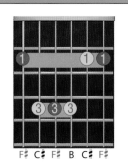

F# C# F# B C# F#

F♯6

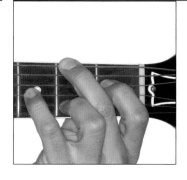

X   X

F#   D# A# C#

F♯7

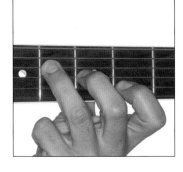
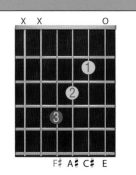

X X   O

F# A# C# E

F♯°7

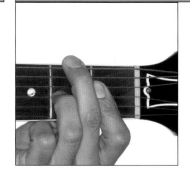
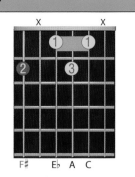

X   X

F#   E♭ A C

F♯9

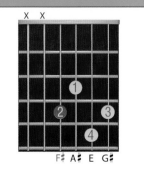

X X

F# A# E G#

F♯13

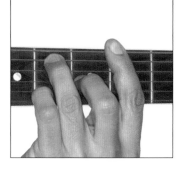
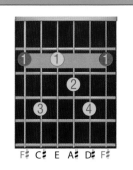

F# C# E A# D# F#

F#maj7

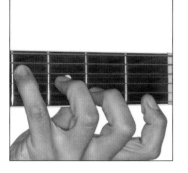
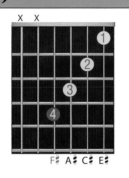

X X

F# A# C# E#

F#m7

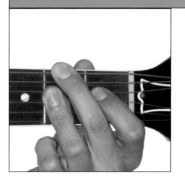

X X

F# E A C#

F#m

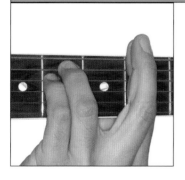
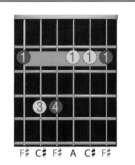

F# C# F# A C# F#

F#m

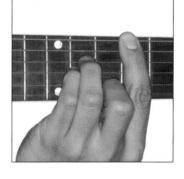
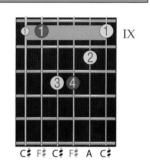

IX

C# F# C# F# A C#

F#m6

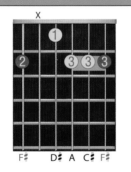

X

F# D# A C# F#

F#m7♭5

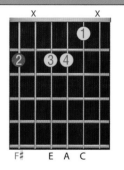

X X

F# E A C

F#m(maj7)

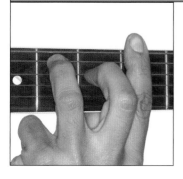

F# C# E# A C# F#

F#m11

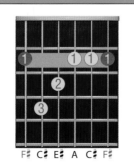

X X O O

F# A B E

Track 10

G major

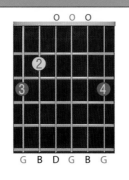
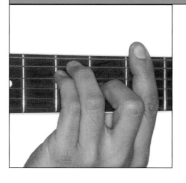

G B D G B G

G major

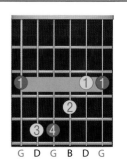

G D G B D G

Gsus4

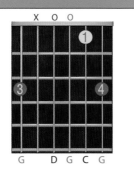

G D G C G

G6

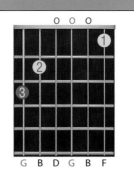
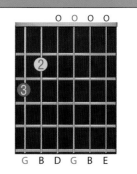

G B D G B E

G7

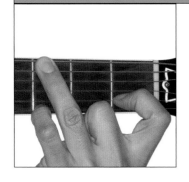
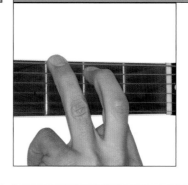

G B D G B F

G°7

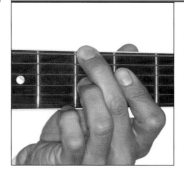
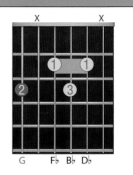

G F♭ B♭ D♭

G9

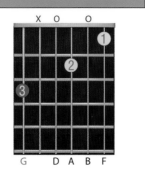

G D A B F

G13

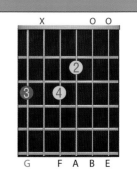

G F A B E

Gmaj7

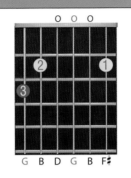

O O O

G B D G B F#

Gm7

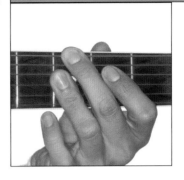

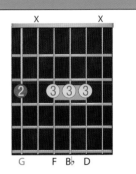

X X

G F Bb D

Gm

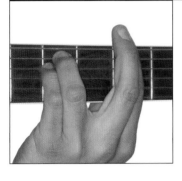

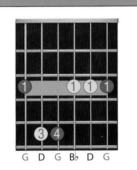

G D G Bb D G

Gm

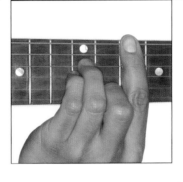

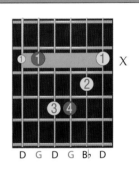

X

D G D G Bb D

Gm6

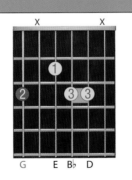

X X

G E Bb D

Gm7b5

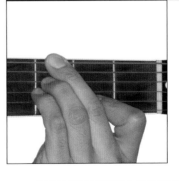

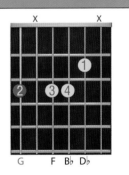

X X

G F Bb Db

Gm(maj7)

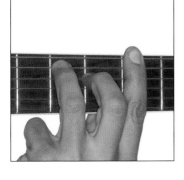

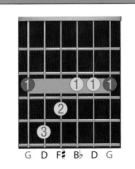

G D F# Bb D G

Gm11

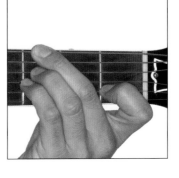

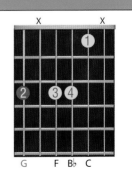

X X

G F Bb C

Track 11

A♭ major

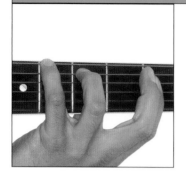
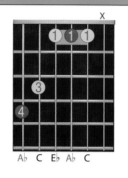

A♭ C E♭ A♭ C

A♭ major

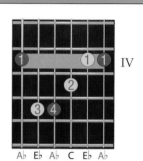
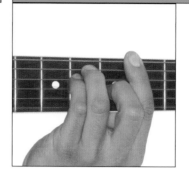

IV

A♭ E♭ A♭ C E♭ A♭

A♭sus4

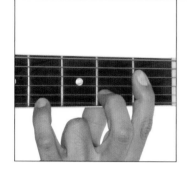
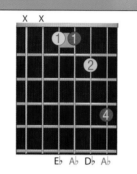

E♭ A♭ D♭ A♭

A♭6

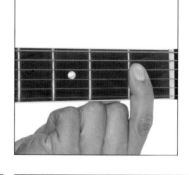

E♭ A♭ C F

A♭7

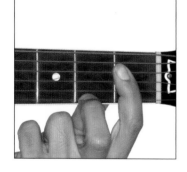
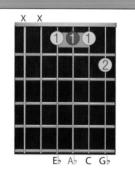

E♭ A♭ C G♭

A♭°7

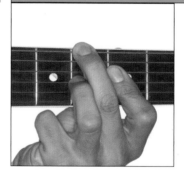
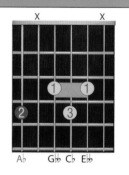

A♭ G♭♭ C♭ E♭♭

A♭9

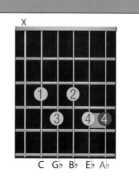

C G♭ B♭ E♭ A♭

A♭13

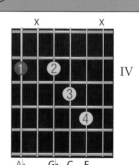

IV

A♭ G♭ C F

A♭maj7

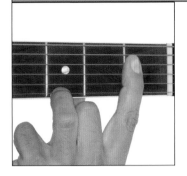

X X
① ① ①
③
E♭ A♭ C G

A♭m7

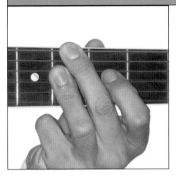
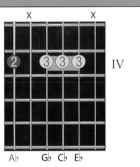

X   X
② ③ ③ ③   IV
A♭   G♭ C♭ E♭

A♭m

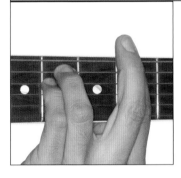
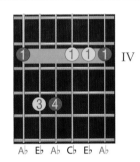

① ① ① ①   IV
A♭ E♭ A♭ C♭ E♭ A♭

A♭m

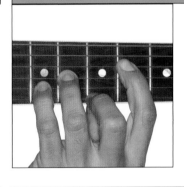
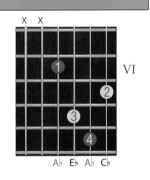

X X
①   VI
②
③
④
A♭ E♭ A♭ C♭

A♭m6

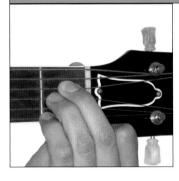
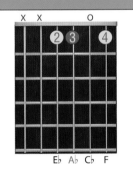

X X   O
② ③   ④
E♭ A♭ C♭ F

A♭m7♭5

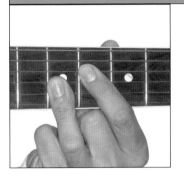
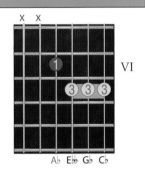

X X
①   VI
③ ③ ③
A♭ E♭ G♭ C♭

A♭m(maj7)

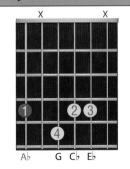

X   X
① ② ③
④
A♭ G C♭ E♭

A♭m11

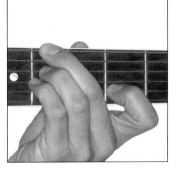
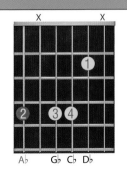

X   X
①
② ③ ④
A♭ G♭ C♭ D♭

Track 12

A major

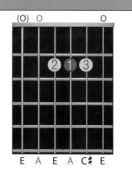

E A E A C# E

A major

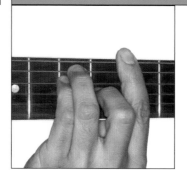

V

A E A C# E A

Asus4

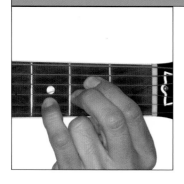
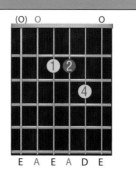

E A E A D E

A6

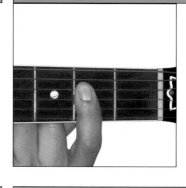
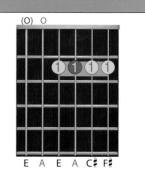

E A E A C# F#

A7

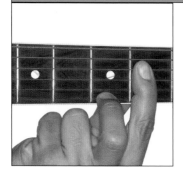
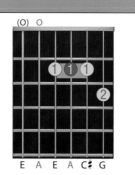

E A E A C# G

A°7

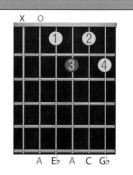

A E♭ A C G♭

A9

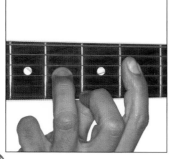
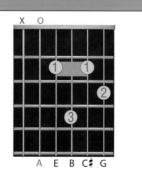

A E B C# G

A13

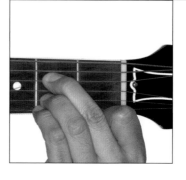
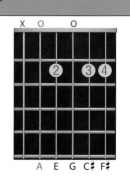

A E G C# F#

Amaj7

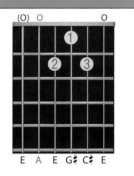
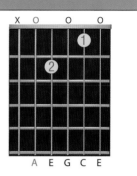

(O) O   O

① ② ③

E A E G♯ C♯ E

Am7

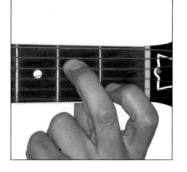

X O O O

① ②

A E G C E

Am

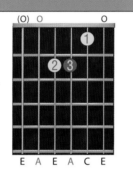

(O) O   O

① ② ③

E A E A C E

Am

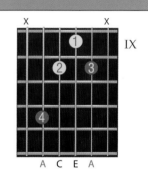

X   X

① ② ③   IX

④

A C E A

Am6

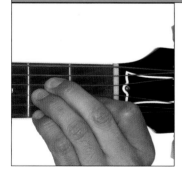
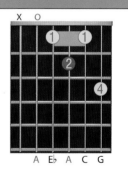

(O) O

① ② ③ ④

E A E A C F♯

Am7♭5

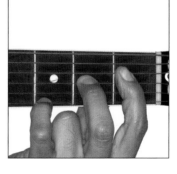
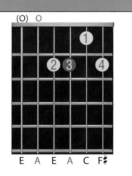

X O

① ① ②

④

A E♭ A C G

Am(maj7)

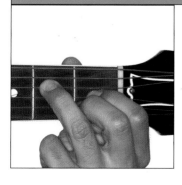
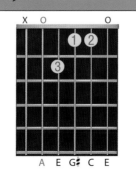

X O   O

① ② ③

A E G♯ C E

Am11

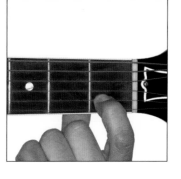
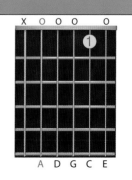

X O O   O

①

A D G C E

Track 13

Bb major

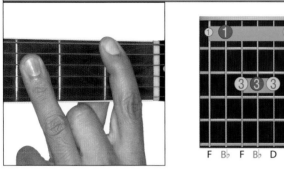

F Bb F Bb D F

Bb major

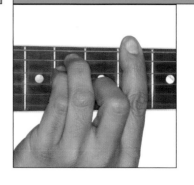

VI

Bb F Bb D F Bb

Bbsus4

F Bb Eb Bb Eb F

Bb6

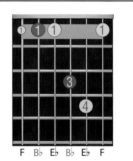

X   O   O

Bb D G D F

Bb7

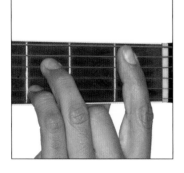

F Bb F Ab D F

Bb°7

X   O   X

Bb Fb Ab Db

Bb9

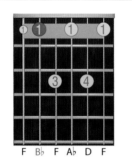

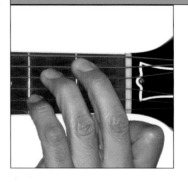

X   O

Bb D Ab C F

Bb13

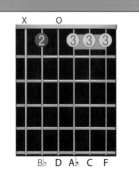

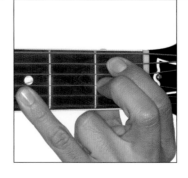

X   X

Bb Ab D G

B♭maj7

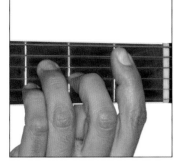

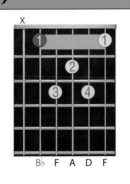

B♭ F A D F

B♭m7

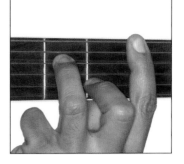

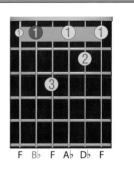

F B♭ F A♭ D♭ F

B♭m

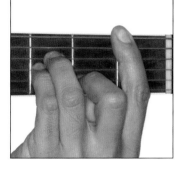

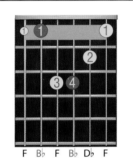

F B♭ F B♭ D♭ F

B♭m

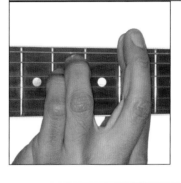

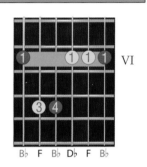

VI

B♭ F B♭ D♭ F B♭

B♭m6

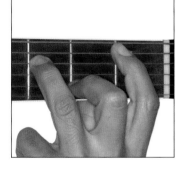

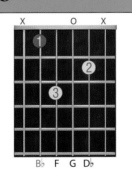

B♭ F G D♭

B♭m7♭5

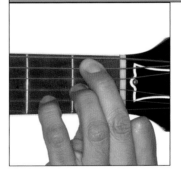

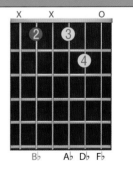

B♭ A♭ D♭ F♭

B♭m(maj7)

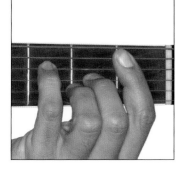

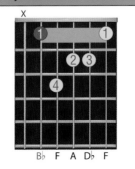

B♭ F A D♭ F

B♭m11

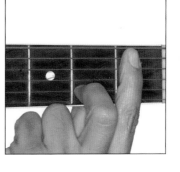

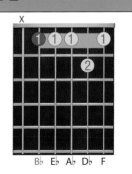

B♭ E♭ A♭ D♭ F

B Chords

B major

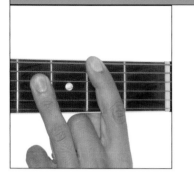
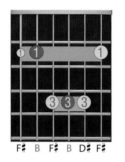

F# B F# B D# F#

B major

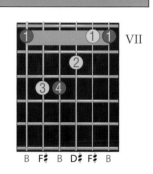

VII

B F# B D# F# B

Bsus4

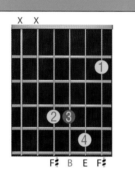

X X

F# B E F#

B6

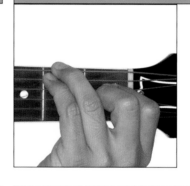
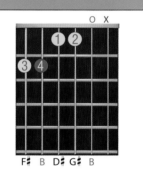

O X

F# B D# G# B

B7

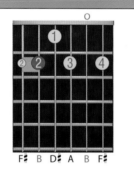

O

F# B D# A B F#

B°7

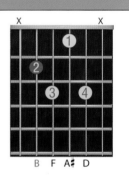

X X

B F A# D

B9

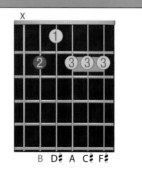

X

B D# A C# F#

B13

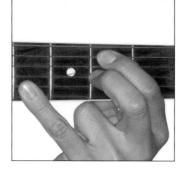
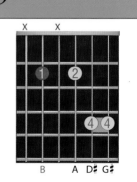

X X

B A D# G#

Bmaj7

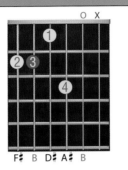

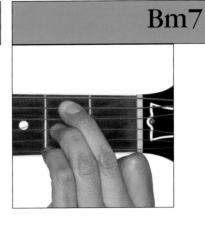

O X

F♯ B D♯ A♯ B

Bm7

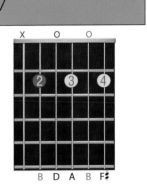

X O O

B D A B F♯

Bm

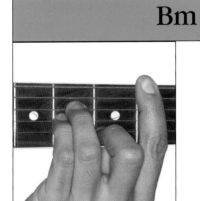

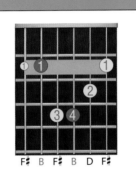

F♯ B F♯ B D F♯

Bm

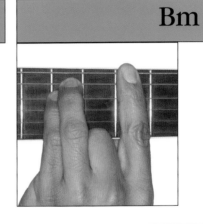

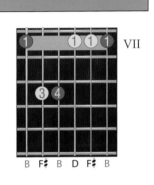

VII

B F♯ B D F♯ B

Bm6

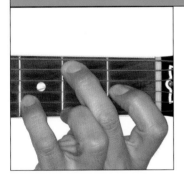

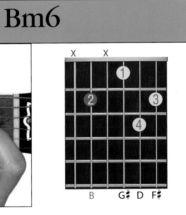

X X

B G♯ D F♯

Bm7♭5

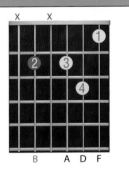

X X

B A D F

Bm(maj7)

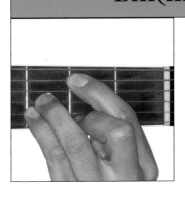

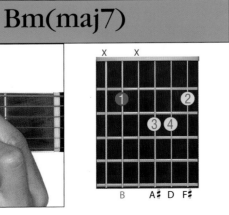

X X

B A♯ D F♯

Bm11

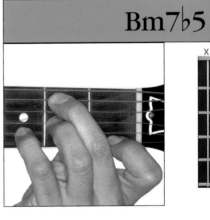

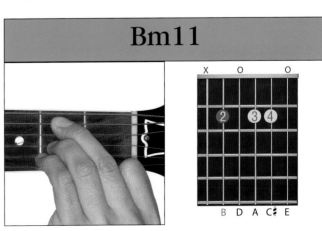

X O O

B D A C♯ E

Special Chords

Track 15 This section consists of chords that are used by many guitarists, but are not really found in too many other chord books. These chords are abbreviated or partial forms. You can use these forms for rhythm or in the construction of lead licks. The chord forms below are known as *5 chords* or *power chords*. These forms are most commonly used in rock, but you will find uses for them in other styles as well.

 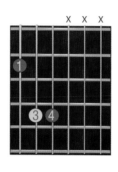 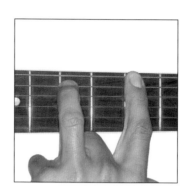 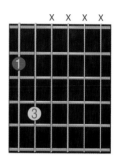

  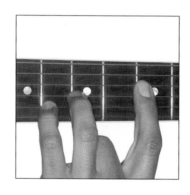 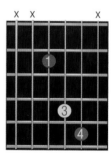

These forms are major and minor triads constructed on the first three strings.

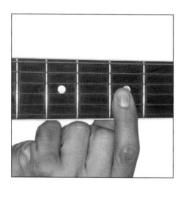 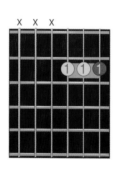  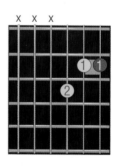

 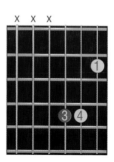  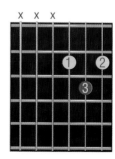

CD contents